WHERE ARCHITECTS STAY AT THE ATLANTIC OCEAN

FRANCE | PORTUGAL | SPAIN

LODGINGS
FOR
DESIGN
ENTHUSIASTS

SIBYLLE KRAMER

WHERE ARCHITECTS STAY AT THE ATLANTIC OCEAN

FRANCE | PORTUGAL | SPAIN

LODGINGS
FOR
DESIGN
ENTHUSIASTS

BRAUN

The Deutsche Nationalbibliothek lists
this publication in the Deutsche National-
bibliografie; detailed bibliographic
data are available on the Internet at
http://dnb.dnb.de

ISBN 978-3-03768-297-5
© 2024 by Braun Publishing AG
www.braun-publishing.ch

1st edition 2024

Editor: Sibylle Kramer
Editorial staff and layout:
Alessia Calabrò
Translation: Benjamin Liebelt
Graphic concept: Michaela Prinz, Berlin
Reproduction: Bild1Druck GmbH, Berlin

Contents

Contents

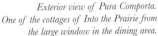
Exterior view of Pura Comporta.
One of the cottages of Into the Prairie from
the large window in the dining area.

Preface

Combining architecture with a vacation is a promising undertaking. Recreation and enjoyment in a consummately shaped environment leaves few wishes unfulfilled. Following the success of the previous volumes, this new book fulfills readers' ongoing desire for another coastal architectural travel guide, this time focusing on the Atlantic region.

The wonderful accommodation presented in this book is as diverse and beautiful as the Atlantic itself. The mighty, majestic ocean has always captivated people with its endless expanse and impetuous waves. At its shores, coastal landscapes of incomparable beauty and diversity have evolved. From wild cliffs to sun-kissed beaches, as well as impressive mountain ranges, the Atlantic coast presents an impressive backdrop for breathtaking architecture. In this environment, the architects' designs not only resist the wind, waves, and salt, but also enable a unique interrelationship between humans and nature. Architectural masterpieces have emerged along the coast in this way, reflecting the beauty and power of the sea. Whether they are minimalist villas that are smoothly integrated into the steep cliff formations, or small cabins, either directly on the beach or in the green hinterland, or even historical lighthouses that proudly rise above the waves – each of these buildings tells a story and inspires the dreams of nature and design lovers.

Cabanas in Comporta nestled in nature. Panoramic view from the terrace of the Akelarre Hotel. Interior view of Le Secret.

For instance the Faro Punta Cumplida lighthouse, on the island of La Palma, with its tall tower and viewing terrace at a height of 34 meters, lets its visitors behold the wild waves crashing upon the cliffs directly beneath them. It is an unforgettable spectacle.

Alternatively, the Villa Pura Comporta, with its broad view of the rural landscape and its impressive architecture, as well as purist rooms and staged vistas, has a decidedly meditative effect. The charming boutique hotel Le Secret on the Île de Ré tells its own story. The architect has applied insight and high-quality design in renovating the historical building, which now radiates all of its former glory.

Each of the presented buildings provides an exceptional quality of stay, allowing visitors to relax and recharge, taking a timeout from the bustle of everyday life. Some will prefer to explore the varied and inspiring coastal cities of La Rochelle, Bilbao, and Lisbon, while others will be attracted to smaller, romantic fishing villages that offer far more than seafood and beautiful sunsets. The selected projects are true gems, imaginatively conceived solitary buildings situated far away from mass tourism. Like a chamber of marvels, this volume whisks lovers of design and travel to the enchanting French, Spanish and Portuguese coasts of the Atlantic Ocean.

INFORMATION. ARCHITECT>
BICA ARQUITECTOS // 2022.
HOUSE> 300 SQM // 12 GUESTS //
6 BEDROOMS // 7 BATHROOMS.
ADDRESS> PENÍNSULA DE TRÓIA,
GRÂNDOLA, PORTUGAL.
WWW.WELCOMEBEYOND.COM/
PROPERTY/COMPORTA-DUNE-HOUSE

House in Tróia

GRÂNDOLA, PORTUGAL

The house is embedded in a landscape of immense natural beauty, facing the sea. The two fundamental principles defining the project were the importance of preserving the environment, specifically protecting the dunes and local vegetation, and ensuring the inhabitants' privacy. Drawing from these ideas, a large dune was carefully formed and covered with native plants surrounding the house. Inside, along a lengthy central corridor, the house's private spaces are arranged symmetrically and interspersed with courtyards filled with already existent greenery, including pines, eucalyptus, and shrubs, which have been retained.

The pool's design anticipates the sea a few meters away. It is accessed via a ramp, covered by a sand-based mortar, to harmonize with the dune landscape. The house's structural solution is based on the resort's principles. It consists of a main load-bearing steel structure with a light steel frame, covered with OSB panels and thermal insulation. The walls have a sand-based mortar finish. Travertine was chosen to complement the range of materials, since the stone resembles the sand layers most closely. The fir and ash wood for the exterior and interior fittings round off the material concept and establish a relationship with the surrounding landscape.

View from above of the terrace with pool. Dining and living area with fireplace. View of the house completely open to the terrace. Exterior view from the pool.

Open kitchen, dining and living area. One bedroom.
Pool from above. Longitudinal section and floor plan.
Aerial view of the house overlooking the ocean.

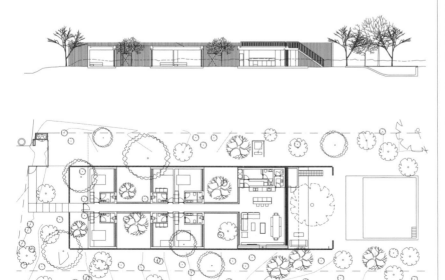

GETTING AROUND. THE HOUSE IS SITUATED ON THE TRÓIA PENÍNSULA, A STRIP OF SAND THAT IS APPROXIMATELY 17 KILOMETERS LONG AND 1.5 KILOMETERS WIDE, SURROUNDED BY SEA. BESIDE THE BEACHES, THE MAIN ATTRACTIONS ARE THE SERRA DA ARRÁBIDA NATURAL PARK, THE BOTANICAL RESERVE OF THE DUNES, AND THE SADO RIVER.

INFORMATION. ARCHITECT>
OLIMPIA ISLA // 2019.
LIGHTHOUSE> 240 SQM //
8 GUESTS // 4 BEDROOMS //
4 BATHROOMS. ADDRESS>
BARLOVENTO, SANTA CRUZ DE
TENERIFE, LA PALMA, SPAIN.
WWW.FLOATEL.DE

Aerial view of Faro Punta Cumplida
surrounded by the ocean. The lighthouse's spiral
staircase. One bedroom with ocean view.

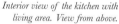

Interior view of the kitchen with living area. View from above.

Faro Punta Cumplida

LA PALMA, SPAIN

There are only very few lighthouses worldwide that offer accommodation. Some of them are very basic, some of them quite luxurious, but all of them are situated in beautiful locations with unique views. Faro Cumplida is the oldest of all and the only one on the Canary Islands that has guest rooms, all while remaining in nautical use.

With its 34-meter-high viewing terrace, it definitively has the highest accessible tower. The views are spectacular and difficult to describe in words. Once you lean against the railing and look at the giant Atlantic waves rolling onto the cliffs more than 50 meters underneath the viewpoint, it becomes difficult to take your eyes off the spectacular scenery. In fact, it is meditation. Time and reality are far away for a moment and only nature is all around you,

allowing you to get very close to true nature.

Faro Punta Cumplida offers three units and can accommodate eight guests. The simple, pure architecture inside the old structure of the lighthouse allows guests to experience the history of the building in a modern context. A local housekeeper takes care of the guests' wishes and prepares a breakfast basket, but the main idea is that they enjoy the lighthouse, the magic of the place, and each other.

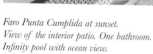

Faro Punta Cumplida at sunset.
View of the interior patio. One bathroom.
Infinity pool with ocean view.

GETTING AROUND. LA ISLA
BONITA OR LA ISLA VERDE IS THE
MOST BEAUTIFUL OF THE CANARY
ISLANDS AND THE NORTHERNMOST,
WITH A WIDE SCENIC AND CLIMATIC
DIVERSITY. IT HAS BEEN DECLARED
A WORLD BIOSPHERE RESERVE AND
STARLIGHT RESERVE. LA PALMA IS
THE IDEAL PLACE FOR SPORTY AND
CULTURALLY INTERESTED TRAVELERS
WHO WISH TO EXPLORE THE ROUGH
COASTLINE, THE LOCAL CUISINE
AND THE INCREDIBLE TRAILS.

INFORMATION. ARCHITECT>
STUDIO 3A // 2019. CABINS>
415 SQM // 8 GUESTS // 4 BEDROOMS
// 8 BATHROOMS. ADDRESS>
BREJOS DA CARREGUEIRA,
COMPORTA, PORTUGAL.
WWW.CO-CABANAS.COM

Cabanas in Comporta

COMPORTA, PORTUGAL

"I want this place to be my retreat. Give me a bed and a bathtub and I'm happy." The Cabanas project in Comporta aims to create a retreat with only the essentials. The project consists of four modules: an intimate zone, a suite, a social area, a living room with a fireplace, a service module, a dining area with a kitchen, and a technical section housing the laundry, storage and garage. The construction system in timber refers to the traditional fishing cabins of the region. In collaboration with Mima Housing, the project was designed to use the advantages of prefabrication.

The house's image is characterized by its finish in charred Douglas fir wood, a sustainable material treated using the Japanese technique shou sugi ban. Not only is it maintenance free, but there are also no toxins or chemicals involved, blending the house with the pine trees. The ventilated roof and the external shading system were important to limit heat absorption. The black cabanas sit invitingly among the wild pine trees.

Kitchen open to the terrace. A cabin nestled in the surrounding nature. View of the terrace with pool. Exterior view of the cabins.

Cozy living room with fireplace. Bathroom.
Exterior view of one cabin at night. Floor plan.
Side view of one cabin.

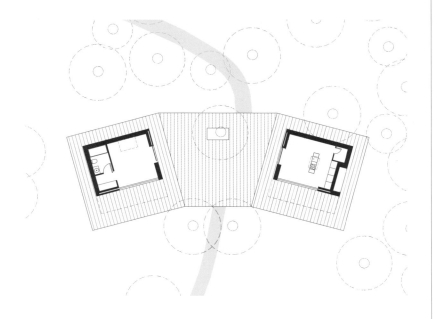

GETTING AROUND. BEYOND THE PINE FOREST AND THE LIMITS OF THE HOUSE, THE RICE FIELDS LIE BETWEEN THE TREES AND THE DUNES. ONE CAN REACH THE ATLANTIC OCEAN IN A FEW MINUTES. THE BEACH HAS A LENGTH OF 45 KILOMETERS, MAKING IT ONE OF THE LONGEST BEACHES IN EUROPE. TO EMBRACE THE COMPORTA LANDSCAPE IS TO BREATHE THE OCEAN BREEZE IN AN ATMOSPHERE OF REFUGE AND MEDITATION. MANY PEOPLE FROM ALL AROUND THE WORLD ENJOY COMPORTA AS THEIR PLACE OF RETREAT: SOMEWHERE TO SHARE AND CREATE THEIR ART, DIVE INTO THE LOCAL CULTURE, AND CONNECT WITH THEMSELVES AND OTHERS. VISITORS ARE INVITED TO PARTICIPATE IN VARIOUS ACTIVITIES SUCH AS SURFING, HIKING, HORSE RIDING AND THE SIMPLE ACT OF ENJOYING THE SUN.

INFORMATION. ARCHITECT> AGENCE BRUNO LE POURVEER // 2016. HOUSES> 135 SQM // 10 GUESTS // 5 BEDROOMS // 3 BATHROOMS. ADDRESS> 12–14 HENT DON KERARZIC, PAIMPOL, FRANCE. WWW.LESPETITESMAISONSARIN.FR

View of living area with window seat overlooking the ocean. Dining area.

Les petites maisons Arin

PAIMPOL, FRANCE

Located in Paimpol, on the Pointe de Kerarzic promontory, this project faces Beauport Abbey. Two adjoining houses have been renovated and the third, in ruins, has been rebuilt. These houses have been restored to their original volumetrics, as their many alterations over the years had seriously undermined the beautiful proportions of these fishing houses.

The unsightly dormers, the augmented volumes, and the retrofitted canopy have been removed, restoring the original beauty of these charming houses. The bays on the south façade have been given more vertical proportions. Each house is once again identifiable by the simple breaks in the roof and the treatment of the façades, which alternate between rendering and stone pointing.

The street-facing gable is now clearly recognizable again, since it sets itself apart from the retaining wall, while its full-width window affords a magnificent view of the abbey.

Exterior view from the garden. View of the kitchen area from the living room.

23

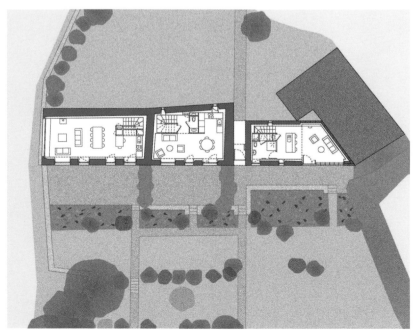

GETTING AROUND. THE SMALL KERARZIC PENINSULA LIES ON THE BOUNDARY BETWEEN TWO EXCEPTIONAL, UNSPOILED LANDSCAPES ON BRITTANY'S NORTHERN COAST: THE BEAUPORT ABBEY ESTATE IN THE BAY OF PAIMPOL AND THE CLIFFS OF THE CÔTE DU GOËLO. THE EXCEPTIONALLY HIGH TIDAL RANGE (UP TO 12 METERS) IN THIS PART OF THE ENGLISH CHANNEL EXPOSES THE VAST FORESHORE OF THE BAY AND GENERATES THE POWERFUL CURRENTS OF THE NEARBY BRÉHAT ARCHIPELAGO.

View of Les petites maisons Arin at sunset.
Floor plan. The garden overlooking the ocean.

Interior view of the living room.
One bathroom. Exterior view.

INFORMATION. ARCHITECT>
CHRISTIAN VON BISMARCK FOR
THE NEW TOWER PROJECT // 1994.
FARMHOUSE> 350 SQM // 9 GUESTS //
4 BEDROOMS // 4 BATHROOMS.
ADDRESS> SOALHEIRA, SÃO BRÁS
DE ALPORTEL, PORTUGAL.
WWW.MONTEDAPALMEIRA.COM

Exterior view. One bedroom of the Terrace Suite.
Living room with fireplace in the Terrace Suite.

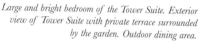

Large and bright bedroom of the Tower Suite. Exterior view of Tower Suite with private terrace surrounded by the garden. Outdoor dining area.

Monte da Palmeira

SÃO BRÁS DE ALPORTEL,
PORTUGAL

Monte da Palmeira is the private estate of an authentic Algarve farmhouse, renting exclusively to groups of guests: a rural hideaway situated above rolling hills, encapsulated by lush gardens and wild nature. Four double bedrooms offer peaceful luxury and timeless style, accommodating up to nine guests.

The fluid, open living spaces feature whitewashed walls and bamboo ceilings, accentuated by dark wood, iron furniture, collectibles, and straw carpets. The two-story, 70-square-meter tower suite features a white and blue bedroom, a lounge area, an en-suite bathroom and a dressing room. The full-marble bathroom includes a tub and private access to the surrounding patio and garden, inviting guests to relax. The patio suite and the 30-square-meter guest house are equally inviting.

The latter is situated 30 meters away from the main building, offering guests privacy and proximity to the pool area, as well as their own patio and a rooftop terrace with a panorama view of the nature reserve and the sea. The lush green grounds include various fruit trees and a herb garden. Many of the corners and niches invite friends and families to gather and eat in the open air, or simply to withdraw.

Main view of the house from the garden with pool.
Interior view of the living room. Detail of the kitchen.
Exterior view.

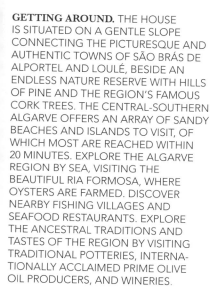

GETTING AROUND. THE HOUSE IS SITUATED ON A GENTLE SLOPE CONNECTING THE PICTURESQUE AND AUTHENTIC TOWNS OF SÃO BRÁS DE ALPORTEL AND LOULÉ, BESIDE AN ENDLESS NATURE RESERVE WITH HILLS OF PINE AND THE REGION'S FAMOUS CORK TREES. THE CENTRAL-SOUTHERN ALGARVE OFFERS AN ARRAY OF SANDY BEACHES AND ISLANDS TO VISIT, OF WHICH MOST ARE REACHED WITHIN 20 MINUTES. EXPLORE THE ALGARVE REGION BY SEA, VISITING THE BEAUTIFUL RIA FORMOSA, WHERE OYSTERS ARE FARMED. DISCOVER NEARBY FISHING VILLAGES AND SEAFOOD RESTAURANTS. EXPLORE THE ANCESTRAL TRADITIONS AND TASTES OF THE REGION BY VISITING TRADITIONAL POTTERIES, INTERNA-TIONALLY ACCLAIMED PRIME OLIVE OIL PRODUCERS, AND WINERIES.

INFORMATION. ARCHITECT>
LAURA ALVAREZ ARCHITECTURE //
2017. HOUSE> 160 SQM // 4 GUESTS //
2 BEDROOMS // 2 BATHROOMS.
ADDRESS> SAN ROQUE DE
RIOMIERA, CANTABRIA, SPAIN.
WWW.VILLASLOW.COM

Frontal view of Villa Slow with closed window doors.
Interior view of a bedroom with en suite shower.

Villa Slow

CANTABRIA, SPAIN

Villa Slow is a rental holiday retreat in the Natural Park of Valles Pasiegos, in the north of Spain. It was created out of a stone ruin within over two hectares of natural countryside around it. The new house type is based on the traditional construction of the area, called "cabaña pasiega" (peasant cabin), but with a contemporary twist. The location of the construction, at the top of a small south-facing hill, affords impressive views toward the valley and mountain.

The floor plan of the house is simple. Two large panoramic windows in the living room, facing opposite directions, create a beautiful backdrop of mountains, clouds, and trees. These two openings allow visitors to enjoy the impressive views towards the valley and mountains from the spacious living room at the center of the house.

Two bedrooms are situated beside the living area, in the eastern wing, on the most private side. Both have their own bathroom and open up toward the endless landscape. The generous room height enables a mezzanine level over the bathroom core for additional sleeping areas. Villa Slow is designed and built with extreme mindfulness and care for detail. The house is very respectful of the environment both regarding aesthetic and technical aspects. Villa Slow is a passive house thanks to a heat pump, under-floor heating, and high-quality insulation and windows, ensuring minimum heat loss.

Interior view of the spacious living room with fireplace. View toward the dining area and kitchen.

GETTING AROUND. LOS VALLES PASIEGOS IS MADE UP OF THREE ADJACENT VALLEYS FORMED BY THE THREE RIVERS THAT GIVE THEM THEIR NAMES: THE PISUEÑA, THE PAS, AND THE MIERA. VILLA SLOW IS LOCATED IN THE MIERA VALLEY. THE THREE VALLEYS ARE SITUATED IN LUSH GREEN TERRAIN. EACH ONE HAS ITS OWN HIDDEN SECRETS, BUT ALL SHARE A UNIQUE ENVIRONMENT, IN WHICH LOCAL TRADITIONS AND CUSTOMS HAVE REMAINED STRONG DESPITE THE PASSAGE OF TIME. THESE ARE THE VALLEYS OF THE PAS REGION, ONE OF THE MOST BEAUTIFUL SPOTS IN CANTABRIA, IN NORTHERN SPAIN.

Exterior view of the house from the garden.
Architectural model. Villa Slow nestled in the
surrounding nature.

View of one bedroom. Detail of the
main entrance. Frontal view of Villa Slow
with open window doors.

INFORMATION. ARCHITECT>
OUTPOST // 2021. 4 HOUSES>
350 SQM // 14 GUESTS //
7 BEDROOMS // 4 BATHROOMS.
ADDRESS> AZENHAS DO MAR,
SINTRA, PORTUGAL.
WWW.OUTPOST.PT

OUTPOST –
Ocean Casitas

SINTRA, PORTUGAL

The four Ocean Casitas are situated at the very top of the whitewashed fishing village of Azenhas do Mar, with a large private patio reaching right to the edge of the cliff. The small houses were fully rebuilt, combining the coziness of the original Portuguese fishing homes with contemporary design, such as open-space layouts, micro-cement flooring, and up to 5-meter-high ceilings.

The spectacular 800 square meters west-facing patio reaches all the way to the vertical cliff. The terrace turned tropical garden is nicely shielded from the predominant north winds by the L-shaped layout of the buildings. The various seating corners along the cliff edge invite guests to enjoy the sunset to the sound of the waves crashing against the rocks 60 meters below.

Living room with fireplace. Large kitchen with dining area. Panoramic view of the ocean. Exterior view.

Outdoor terrace with ocean view. Details of the bedroom furniture. Floor plans. Interior view of one bright bedroom.

GETTING AROUND. THE OCEAN CASITAS IN THE FISHING VILLAGE OF AZENHAS DO MAR ARE LOCATED ONLY 40 KILOMETERS FROM LISBON. A SHORT WALK LEADS ALONG WINDING PATHS AND UP STEPS TO THE NATURAL OCEAN POOL. SEVERAL BEACHES ARE IN THE DIRECT VICINITY, INCLUDING THE "HOME BEACH" ONLY A FIVE-MINUTE WALK AWAY.

INFORMATION. ARCHITECT> ATELIER D'ARCHITECTURE GARDERA-PASTRE // 2022. HOTEL> 1,100 SQM // 20 BEDROOMS // 20 BATHROOMS. ADDRESS> 3 ESPLANADE DU PORT VIEUX, BIARRITZ, AQUITAINE, BIARRITZ, FRANCE. WWW.HOTELDELAPLAGE-BIARRITZ.COM

Exterior view of the hotel from the beach. View of the exterior façade. Interior view of one bedroom.

Hôtel de la Plage

BIARRITZ, FRANCE

Biarritz's legendary Hôtel de la Plage reopened its doors in June 2022, following extensive refurbishment. Located on Biarritz's Port Vieux, the hotel offers a breathtaking view of the Rocher de la Vierge, accessible by foot via a footbridge. The hotel's architecture was inspired by the site's brutalist and Art Deco tones, and in particular by the stone arches that characterize the old port's beach enclosure.

The 20 rooms are spread over three levels and accessed by a wide central staircase along a landscaped, south-facing patio that bathes the common areas in abundant natural light. An accessible rooftop offers a festive terrace with a breathtaking view of the ocean and the Rocher de la Vierge footbridge. Inside, the hotel's design codes assume the fresh, "surf and sun", cheerful feel of the Basque coast. A specially designed, undulating wooden ceiling covers the entire ground floor, including the reception area, restaurant, and library. Sandy tones dominate the communal areas, while the rooms draw their identity from a subtle interplay of color, based on the shades of the surrounding landscape, the blues of the sea, and the greens of the mountains.

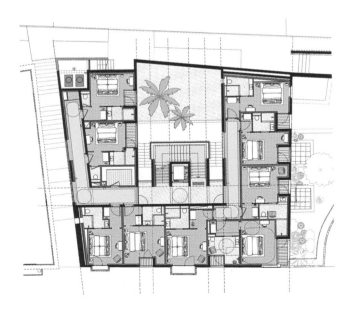

GETTING AROUND. BIARRITZ, THE JEWEL OF THE BASQUE COAST AND A FORMER FISHING TOWN PRIZED FOR ITS FINE SANDY BEACHES AND GENEROUS WAVES, IS ALSO LOCATED AT THE FOOT OF THE PYRENEES MOUNTAINS, OFFERING HIKING TRAILS AND SKI SLOPES IN WINTER JUST ONE HOUR AWAY BY CAR. THE CITY'S CULTURAL OFFERINGS ARE UNMATCHED: THE MUSÉE DE LA MER, THE MUSÉE ASIATICA, THE CITÉ DE L'OCÉAN, AND THE PALAIS DES FESTIVALS ARE ESSENTIAL VISITS, BEFORE ENJOYING AN EVENING APERITIF IN ONE OF THE MANY TAPAS BARS LINING THE HALLES DISTRICT.

Exterior view of Hôtel de la Plage. Floor plan.
Interior of one room with ocean view.

Interior view of one bedroom. Common living area.
Ocean view from the rooftop terrace.

INFORMATION. ARCHITECT>
MEZZO ATELIER // 2017.
HOUSE AND STUDIO> 288 SQM //
7 GUESTS // 3 BEDROOMS //
4 BATHROOMS. ADDRESS>
RUA JOSÉ MEDEIROS COGUMBREIRO
N 67, PONTA DELGADA, AZORES
ISLANDS, PORTUGAL.
WWW.PINKHOUSEAZORES.PT

Pink House

AZORES ISLANDS, PORTUGAL

On the Atlantic island of São Miguel, an old stable was converted into two guesthouses, where tradition and modernity coexist in mutual harmony. The design kept the construction's character and its rural atmosphere, while adapting it to a completely new typology and contemporary needs. New apertures were carefully incised into the pink colored façades, as well as in the stone wall, while a new volume was added to the main construction, allowing a second, smaller house to appear integrated into the ensemble.

The larger house develops on two levels: the ground floor opens up to the surrounding exterior spaces, creating a mezzanine hallway that provides access to the private suites. On the upper floor, the social areas benefit from the beautiful pitched roof's old structure. Several elements in the project are reinterpretations of the local vernacular architecture, which was an important source of inspiration and reference.

Exterior view from the terrace. Kitchen and dining room. Living room with window seat. View of the Pink House from the street.

Front view from the inner courtyard. Studio's kitchen.
View of one terrace. Floor plans. Interior view from
the double-height living area.

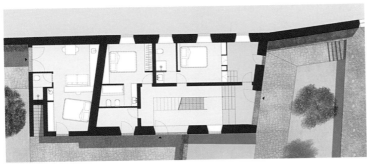

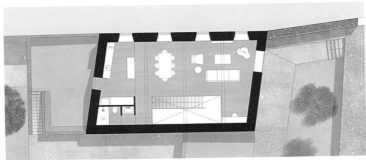

GETTING AROUND. PINK HOUSE IS LOCATED IN A VERY CENTRAL AREA ON THE ISLAND, BETWEEN THE CITY OF PONTA DELGADA AND RIBEIRA GRANDE, BUT ALSO VERY CLOSE TO BLACK SANDY BEACHES SUCH AS SANTA BARBARA, THE BREATHTAKING LAGOONS OF SETE CIDADES AND LAGOA DO FOGO, AND THE WATERFALLS AND THERMAL BATHS IN FURNAS VALLEY, ALL OF WHICH ARE REACHABLE IN AROUND 30-40 MINUTES. VISITS TO THE TEA AND PINEAPPLE PLANTATIONS ARE A MUST. DIVING AND WHALE WATCHING CAN ALSO BE MEMORABLE EXPERIENCES WHILE STAYING ON THE ISLAND.

INFORMATION. ARCHITECTS>
BENEDICT AND CATHERINE AGNEW //
2017. HOUSE> 65 SQM // 5 GUESTS //
2 BEDROOMS // 1 BATHROOM.
ADDRESS> LA PEÑA, TARIFA, SPAIN.
WWW.TARIFABEACHHOUSES.COM/
PROPERTY/LITTLE-STONE-HOUSE/

*Main view of the house. View of the kitchen. Interior
view of the dining and living area. The Little Stone
House surrounded by nature.*

Little Stone House

TARIFA, SPAIN

The Little Stone House is an enchanting shepherd's cabin that was fully renovated in 2017. Positioned at the top of the La Pena hillside, the house enjoys incredible 360° views of Los Lances beach below and the protected cork forest and mountains above. It is ideal for a couple or family of up to five people. The house itself has a size of 65 square meters and includes an open-plan sitting room, dining room, kitchen, double bedroom, bunk room, and bathroom.

The kitchen is well-equipped with a four-hob gas stove, oven, and large fridge-freezer. There is also a Weber gas BBQ for outside grilling. The sitting room has a large sofa and chaise longe, as well as a wild olive dining table for eight people, and benches to enjoy the sea views. The stone terrace offers a shaded seating area, outdoor eating for six, a BBQ area, and a shower. The views from inside and outside the building are breathtaking. At night, the house resembles an alpine lodge, with its contemporary finish, elegant wooden-beamed roofs, and stylish black-framed glass. There is a chlorinated dipping pool for guests' exclusive use beside the house.

The Little Stone House with ocean view.
Interior view of one bedroom.

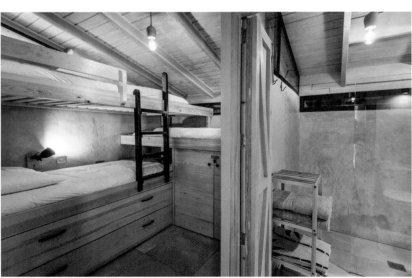

Main bedroom. Front view of the house.
Interior view of the bathroom.

GETTING AROUND. THE NEIGHBOR RAFAEL HAS HIS GENTLE DONKEY GRAZING ON THE PLOT OUT OF SEASON AND OFTEN A STRAY PIG LOOKS UP AT THE KITCHEN WINDOW. IT IS VERY MUCH FOR NATURE LOVERS AND GUESTS WHO ARE LOOKING TO ENJOY WALKS FROM THE PROPERTY, ON THE MANY FORESTRY TRACKS AND THE SOMEWHAT INFAMOUS BUDDHA TRAIL, WHICH IS NOT FAR AWAY. THE HOUSE'S PROXIMITY TO THE BEACH (750 METERS) AND THE TOWN (6 KILOMETERS) IS WHAT MAKES LA PENA SUCH A POPULAR LOCATION, A VERY SPECIAL CHOICE FOR A FAMILY OR COUPLE WANTING TO GET AWAY FROM IT ALL AND RECONNECT WITH NATURE.

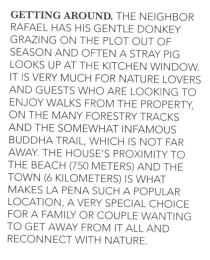

INFORMATION. ARCHITECTS>
DEPA – LUÍS SOBRAL, CARLOS
AZEVEDO, JOÃO CRISÓSTOMO
AND ÂNGELA MEIRELES // 2021.
TOWNHOUSE> 326 SQM // 16 GUESTS
// 8 BEDROOMS // 9 BATHROOMS.
ADDRESS> TRAVESSA DE SÃO
SEBASTIÃO 39, PORTO, PORTUGAL.
WWW.NATRAVESSA.COM

*Exterior view from the courtyard. Room with city
view. One bedroom with private bathroom.*

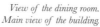
View of the dining room.
Main view of the building.

Na Travessa Suítes

PORTO, PORTUGAL

The Travessa building is located in Morro da Sé, in the heart of the historical center of Porto, classified as UNESCO World Heritage. The urban fabric it integrates has a strong historical and monumental value for the city of Porto.

The block is mostly made up of buildings with a traditional character and matrix. Despite their architectural homogeneity, they shape the city's identity. Thus, in implementing the conversion, the architects were interested in highlighting the building's qualities, which they had identified as original and characteristic elements. These included the front facade and its masonry, the balconies, the iron guardrails, and the portals on the ground floor that connect with the patio.

The project impressively demonstrates how a good conversion measure can work by grasping the building's history and conceiving modifications that harmonize with the surroundings.

Common seating area with glass windows overlooking the inner courtyard. Interior view of one bedroom. Detail of the interior staircase. Floor plans.

GETTING AROUND. THE HISTORICAL CITY OF PORTO IS RELATIVELY SMALL. WALKING THROUGH THE NARROW STREETS, YOU WILL FIND BEAUTIFUL CHURCHES COVERED IN TYPICAL TILES, TRADITIONAL SHOPS, SMALL BARS, AND EXCELLENT RESTAURANTS. SÃO BENTO STATION, THE CLÉRIGOS TOWER, SÉ CATHEDRAL AND THE D. LUÍS I BRIDGE DESIGNED BY GUSTAVE EIFFEL ARE PLACES NOT TO BE MISSED. ON THE OTHER SIDE OF THE BRIDGE, ENJOY THE MOST BEAUTIFUL SUNSETS AND VIEWS OVER THE RIVER AND THE OLD CITY, WHILE PLANNING A VISIT TO THE PORT'S WINE CELLARS. SERRALVES MUSEUM BY ÁLVARO SIZA VIEIRA AND CASA DA MÚSICA BY REM KOOLHAAS ARE TWO EXAMPLES OF MODERN ARCHITECTURE IN PORTO.

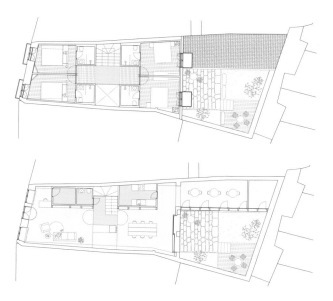

INFORMATION. ARCHITECT>
ATELIER RUA // 2019.
HOUSE> 600 SQM // 10 GUESTS //
5 BEDROOMS // 6 BATHROOMS.
ADDRESS> ALVIQUER, TAVIRA,
PORTUGAL.
WWW.HOSPEDARIA.COM.PT

Covered terrace with seating area. Top view of the triangular plot. Interior view of the living room.

Hospedaria

TAVIRA, PORTUGAL

The property is situated in a rural area near the city of Trevia, at the junction between three municipal roads. On this inhospitable, triangular lot, which is completely surrounded by roads, two old buildings were carefully restored using traditional building methods, recreating their original character and preserving their cozy atmosphere.

Five new volumes were built on the remaining area. Each of the bedrooms has its own patio, while the rooms' organization was individually tailored according to the situation, light, and existing trees. The interior ceilings are in exposed concrete, while the windows now open generously to enable an extension of the interior into the private patios.

The new volumes are also strategically embedded in the lot in order to define four new patios with a more public character, thus defining different environments and degrees of privacy.

GETTING AROUND. TAVIRA IS A CITY BRIMMING WITH HISTORY AND NATURAL SPLENDOR. ITS ROMAN BRIDGE SPANS THE GILÃO RIVER, OFFERING VISTAS OF THE OLD TOWN'S WHITEWASHED BUILDINGS AND NARROW STREETS. THE NEARBY RIA FORMOSA NATURE RESERVE IS TEEMING WITH WILDLIFE. VISITORS TO THIS COASTAL PARADISE CAN ENJOY THE SCENERY ON WALKS THROUGH THE SALT MARSHES AND DUNES, AS WELL AS THE UNTOUCHED BEACHES. ONLY A FEW KILOMETERS AWAY, THE PICTURESQUE VILLAGE OF CACELA VELHA IS PERCHED UPON THE CLIFF. THE BREATHTAKING VIEWS, THE EXQUISITE OYSTERS AND FANTASTIC SUNSETS ARE ALL EXCEPTIONAL.

Interior view of the dining area.
Floor plan. Covered terrace.

One bedroom. Living room with
fireplace. Exterior view.

INFORMATION. ARCHITECT>
JÉRÔME PERRIN // 1885,
RENOVATION 2020. BOUTIQUE
HOTEL> 250 SQM // 10 GUESTS //
5 BEDROOMS // 5 BATHROOMS.
ADDRESS> 21 AVENUE VICTOR
BOUTHILLIER, SAINT MARTIN
DE RE, FRANCE.
WWW.LESECRETDERE.COM

Le Secret

SAINT MARTIN DE RE,
FRANCE

The charming new boutique hotel in an 1885 residence by the port of Saint Martin, the capital of the Île de Ré, with a large, quiet garden and trees, offers a heated swimming pool and wellness services available on request. Five rooms are equipped with WiFi and very tasteful furnishing. You enter a house steeped in history, with a magnificently preserved architectural ensemble. The location is ideal near the port of Saint Martin and at the heart of the village, but sheltered from the hustle and bustle, with a large walled garden, facing south, to ensure privacy.

The owners live there themselves and are happy to share their passion for the island, its secret routes, good places, and unusual itineraries. The house was conceived as a peaceful, friendly place that focuses on beautiful books and warm aperitifs. Completely renovated, the house has regained its radiance and preserved its moldings, woodwork, parquet floors, fireplaces, and porcelain basin, all the architectural riches of the time. Choose from five spacious rooms, each unique and equipped with a shower room. The particularly neat furniture combines classic and contemporary styles.

Chambre Alcôve with en suite bathroom. Interior view. Study corner with stained glass windows. Interior view of Chambre Prélude with fireplace.

Interior view of the kitchen with dining area.
Chambre Fugue living area.

Sleeping area of Chambre Fugue on the mezzanine.
En suite bathroom of Chambre Volute. Interior view
of Chambre Volute.

GETTING AROUND. THE HOUSE IS ON THE PORT OF SAINT MARTIN, CAPITAL OF THE ÎLE DE RÉ. IT IS AN OASIS OF SERENITY FOR YOU TO RELAX AFTER COVERING MILES BY BIKE, ON FOOT, OR SWIMMING. THE HOUSE IS SITUATED IN THE MIDDLE OF THE ISLAND WITH 200 KILOMETERS OF CYCLE PATHS ALL AROUND. THE SEA IS EVERYWHERE, ALLOWING VISITORS TO CHOOSE A SPOT ANYWHERE ALONG THE OVER 0 KILOMETERS OF BEACH. SAINT MARTIN VILLAGE IS IN THE MIDDLE OF A 17TH-CENTURY FORTRESS, OFFERING A WEALTH OF LOCAL PRODUCTION: HAND-MADE SEA SALT, OYSTERS, SOAP MADE OF DONKEY'S MILK, AND MUCH MORE.

INFORMATION. ARCHITECT>
NUNO NASCIMENTO ARCHITECTURE
// 2022. GUESTHOUSE> 130 SQM //
6 GUESTS // 3 BEDROOMS //
3 BATHROOMS. ADDRESS>
VALE DO LOBO, ALMANCIL,
ALGARVE, PORTUGAL.
WWW.DESIGN-ESCAPES.COM/
CASA-DA-AOTEIA

*Aerial view of Casa da Açoteia. Interior view
from the entrance. Dining area.*

Casa da Açoteia

ALMANCIL, PORTUGAL

Casa da Açoteia is a holiday house in Vale do Lobo, a tourist resort in the Algarve, in the south of Portugal. The project's aim was to renovate one of the oldest houses in the resort, giving it a new "barefoot luxury". The house consists of three floors: the first with the social areas and one suite, the second with two suites, and the third with the "Açoteia", the Portuguese definition of a small rooftop terrace. The archetype is mostly found in Algarve, as it was a space typically used for drying fruit. In recent decades, these spaces have been turned into leisure areas, as is the case with the Casa da Açoteia: It invites guests to relax, refresh and recharge.

The building concept thrives on the continuity of its materials. The ceilings, walls, and floors are continuous, with white handmade plaster covering all surfaces. Thus, the house feels fresh in the hottest days of summer, but the inclusion of natural wood elements such as doors and cabinets make the spaces still feel comfortable all year long.

GETTING AROUND. NESTLED IN THE CAPTIVATING COASTAL LANDSCAPE OF ALMANCIL, PORTUGAL, LIES THE ENCHANTING VALE DO LOBO. HERE, PICTURESQUE CLIFFS CASCADE INTO GOLDEN SHORES, FRAMED BY AZURE WATERS THAT WHISPER TALES OF TIMELESS ELEGANCE. THE SEA WITH ITS ENDLESS BEACHES IS VERY NEAR, INVITING VISITORS TO A WIDE RANGE OF ACTIVITIES AND RELAXATION. FARO, ALBUFEIRA, AND MANY OTHER BEAUTIFUL TOWNS AND LOCATIONS ARE ONLY HALF AN HOUR AWAY BY CAR.

View of the living room with large curved sofa.
Floor plans. Detail of the sofa area.

View of the terrace with pool.
One bedroom. Interior view of the kitchen.

INFORMATION. ARCHITECT>
SUSANNE GERSTBERGER,
MONOSTUDIO // 2013. HOUSE>
100 SQM // 6 GUESTS // 3 BEDROOMS
// 2 BATHROOMS. ADDRESS>
ADAN CAZORLA VALERON 25,
MOGAN, GRAN CANARIA, SPAIN.
WWW.FINCA-PARAISO.COM

*The entrance of Finca Paraiso. Shower with
natural rock face. View of the dining area.*

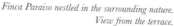
*Finca Paraiso nestled in the surrounding nature.
View from the terrace.*

Finca Paraiso

GRAN CANARIA, SPAIN

Finca Paraiso is a small country house in the local style of the Canary Isles, which has been extended with elements of modern, minimalist architecture. The interior's specific design language has transformed it into a modern residence. Comprising around 100 square meters, the house is divided into a large living area with an integrated designer kitchen, three double bedrooms and a natural stone bathroom specially designed for the house.

Each of the three double rooms has its own style: The "Tabaiba Room" is regarded as a small, independent suite. It has its own bathroom and a separate entrance via the mosaic patio. It can easily accommodate a small child's bed. The "Classic Room" and the "Vintage Room" share the wonderful natural stone bathroom, where one showers beside the rock face, beneath the open, blue sky.

The differently designed patios, which are oriented in various directions, fulfill a variety of individual requirements. On the panorama patio (part of the house), you can let the stress of everyday life melt away. The mosaic patio "behind" the house allows you to wonder at the hills in peace and quiet. The shadiest patio provides shelter from the heat and sun, its fig tree making a perfect spot for readers. The sunbathing patio has comfortable recliners to relax on.

Interior view of the kitchen and dining room with large panoramic window. Exterior view from the terrace at night.

Detail of the outdoor seating alcove. View of the "Vintage Room". View of the kitchen island.

GETTING AROUND. THE LOCATION IN THE SUNNY SOUTH OF GRAN CANARIA, WITH AROUND 340 DAYS OF SUNSHINE A YEAR, OFFERS A WIDE RANGE OF SPORTS AND LEISURE ACTIVITIES. IT IS IDEAL FOR CYCLISTS AND RAMBLERS, SINCE THE FINCA IS SITUATED DIRECTLY ON A MOUNTAIN TRAIL THAT IS ESPECIALLY POPULAR IN THE WINTER MONTHS. GRAN CANARIA IS A PERFECT DESTINATION FOR WATER SPORTS ENTHUSIASTS DUE TO ITS MILD CLIMATE ALL YEAR ROUND. THERE ARE ALSO SEVERAL GOLF COURSES WITHIN A 20-MINUTE DRIVE.

INFORMATION. ARCHITECT>
GUILHERME MACHADO VAZ // 2018.
HOUSE> 165 SQM // 6 GUESTS //
3 BEDROOMS // 3 BATHROOMS.
ADDRESS> CAMINHO DE
PARANHOS 289, AFIFE, VIANA
DO CASTELO, PORTUGAL.
WWW.GUILHERMEMACHADOVAZ.PT

Main view of the house from the garden with swimming pool. Interior view of the kitchen area open to the garden.

House in Afife

VIANA DO CASTELO,
PORTUGAL

The house is situated in the north of Portugal, in a rural, coastal settlement. A path separates the plot from a chapel. The designers sought not to disturb the harmony of this religious space, but at the same time it did not want to be submissive to its presence. A square footprint was defined and repeated in the swimming pool, as well as in the space between both.

The regular volume, compact and vertical, evokes the essence of a traditional construction type. The project follows the natural topography of the land. The building was adapted to the terrain through mezzanine levels, which allowed a direct relationship between interior and exterior areas, despite maintaining a strong aesthetic contrast between them.

The façade functions as a shell that allows communication between the house and the surroundings by opening the blinds.

Exterior view of House in Afife.
The living room.

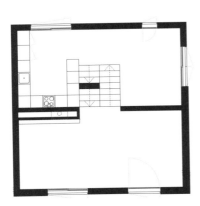

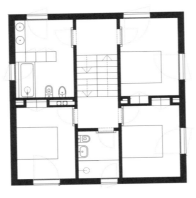

GETTING AROUND. AFIFE IS A GREAT OLD VILLAGE TO DISCOVER ON FOOT AND IS CLOSE TO TOWNS WITH IMPORTANT CULTURAL AND ARCHITECTURAL HERITAGE. THE HOUSE IS LOCATED BETWEEN THE OCEAN AND THE HILLS, ALLOWING A WIDE VARIETY OF ACTIVITIES, SUCH AS SURFING AND HIKING. THE BEAUTIFUL MINHO RIVER CAN ALSO BE EXPLORED. SPAIN IS ON THE OPPOSITE BANK. WONDERFUL RESTAURANTS ALSO OFFER FRESH FISH AND SEAFOOD, AS WELL AS LOCAL DELICACIES.

Exterior view from the street. Ground and first floor plan. The swimming pool.

View from above. Detail of the open wooden staircase. The house surrounded by greenery.

INFORMATION. ARCHITECT>
PHILIPPE RIZZOTTI ARCHITECTE //
2019. VILLA> 420 SQM // 14 GUESTS //
7 BEDROOMS // 4 BATHROOMS.
ADDRESS> IMPASSE DE CAYOLA 93,
TALMONT-SAINT-HILAIRE, FRANCE.
WWW.VILLACAYOLA.FR

Villa Cayola

TALMONT-SAINT-HILAIRE,
FRANCE

This small, autonomous, prefabricated, modular, and durable haven of peace is embedded in the vegetation on the edge of the Atlantic Ocean. Based on the locally typical Longères architecture and the peculiarity of the property located in the second row facing the sea, the ensemble is composed of three identical volumes of 6 x 12 meters, covering an area of 240 square meters.

The project's organization is based on a square module containing and organizing the seven bedrooms, with sizes varying from 18 to 22 square meters, as well as two large living rooms and an indoor swimming pool, each with a size of 66 square meters. The three building wings form the boundary beyond which the wooded areas remain in their natural state and are accessible according to the buildings' orientation. All rooms have a wide open view toward the pine forests in the east, thereby also enjoying the morning sun.

Exterior view of Villa Cayola. Outdoor area directly on the beach. Front view. Interior view of the dining room and kitchen.

View of the villa from the beach. Indoor swimming pool. View of the staircase. First floor plan. Main entrance of Villa Cayola.

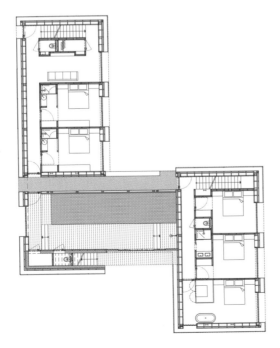

GETTING AROUND. THE VICINITY OFFERS THE BEACHES LA PLAGE DU VEILLON AND LA PLAGE DE TANCHET, PORT BOURGENAY GOLF CLUB, THE VENDÉE AQUARIUM, THE PORT OF BOURGENAY, LES SABLES-D'OLONNE ZOO, AN AUTOMOBILE MUSEUM, AND A CASINO. VISITORS CAN ALSO ENJOY ACTIVITIES SUCH AS SURFING, PARACHUTING, PADDLING, KAYAKING, KITE SURFING, CYCLING, TENNIS, AND HORSE RIDING.

INFORMATION. ARCHITECT>
PAR – PLATAFORMA DE
ARQUITECTURA // 2015.
HOUSE> 350 SQM // 16 GUESTS //
8 BEDROOMS // 12 BATHROOMS.
ADDRESS> QUATRIM DO SUL,
OLHÃO, ALGARVE, PORTUGAL.
WWW.CASAMODESTA.PT

Exterior view of the stairs leading to the
rooftop. Interior view of one bedroom. View
of the outdoor area.

Exterior view of Casa Modesta.
Exterior staircases.

Casa Modesta

OLHÃO, PORTUGAL

Casa Modesta always welcomes its visitors with open arms. The project was inspired by the grandfather of the family, the "old sea dog" Joaquim Modesto de Brito, also known to all as "the champ". So many memories inhabit these walls and grounds that the grandchildren refused to let them disappear.

This is how Casa Modesta was born, combining rural tourism with a contemporary feel, manifested in eight rooms with private patios. There is also a garden with a section for organically grown vegetables and a solarium where time passes with the tides.

The design combines traditional knowledge with the region's architectural culture, referring to the local people and materials. Anchored in the memory of the family and its location, Casa Modesta is a special place to visit.

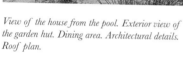

View of the house from the pool. Exterior view of the garden hut. Dining area. Architectural details. Roof plan.

GETTING AROUND. THE FAMILY HOUSE OPENS ITS DOORS TO TOURISM IN AN ALMOST UNKNOWN AREA, FACING THE SEA AND SITUATED IN THE HEART OF THE RIA FORMOSA NATURE PARK, WHICH IS CONSIDERED ONE OF PORTUGAL'S SEVEN WONDERS. FROM CASA MODESTA, VISITORS CAN MARVEL AT THE MIGRATION OF BIRDS AND THE SALT HARVESTING, AS WELL AS ADMIRING THE SMALL WONDERS THAT NATURE PERFORMS EVERY DAY.

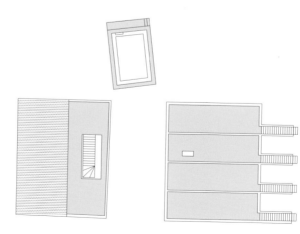

INFORMATION. ARCHITECTS> GONZALO CONDE LOBATO AND CARLOS ROMERO LAGE // 2016. HOUSE> 130 SQM // 5 GUESTS // 3 BEDROOMS // 3 BATHROOMS. ADDRESS> CAMBRE 16, CARBALLO, A CORUÑA, SPAIN. WWW.VILANOVAA.COM

Interior view of one bedroom with en suite shower. Exterior view of the façade overlooking the ocean.

Mirador das Areas

A CORUÑA, SPAIN

The Mirador das Areas is a unique refuge, in a small rural area of stone houses, which has a privileged location, facing the sea, in the protected natural area of Razo Baldaio. The building has a total size of 130 square meters, distributed over three floors: the ground floor, upper floor and attic. The small private garden includes a plunge-pool. Everywhere, one can enjoy the spectacular views of the Atlantic Ocean.

Respect for tradition and maximum comfort go hand in hand in this house. It has been completely renovated, with a modern feel, always respecting its natural identity. The stone walls and recovered hardwood floors have been restored in a traditional way. Old doors and the century-old gallery that frames the spectacular views have also been recovered. One can enjoy a simple vacation like a local in this Galician natural paradise.

Main view of the house from the street.
Razo Baldaio beach in front of the house.

GETTING AROUND. WALKING DOWN TO ONE OF THE BEST BEACHES IN SPAIN, THROUGH THE PATHS BETWEEN THE DUNES, IS A REAL PLEASURE. COSTA DA MORTE, SURROUNDED BY FORESTS, LIGHT-HOUSES, CLIFFS, AND WILD BEACHES WITH DUNES, OFFERS EXCELLENT SURFING, CYCLING, AND HORSE RIDING OPPORTUNITIES. MANY SIGHT-SEEING ATTRACTIONS AND SERVICES ARE AVAILABLE NEARBY, INCLUDING CABALLO (10 MINUTES), A CORUÑA (30 MINUTES), SANTIAGO DE COMPOSTELA (55 MINUTES), AND FISTERRA (1 HOUR).

Bedroom with bathtub and ocean view. Section. Outdoor terrace.

View of living room with kitchen and dining area. Panoramic view from one bedroom terrace. View of one bedroom.

INFORMATION. ARCHITECT>
MANUEL AIRES MATEUS // 1728,
RENOVATION 2016. HOUSE>
1,115 SQM // 16 GUESTS //
6 SUITES // 7 BATHROOMS.
ADDRESS> CAMPO DE SANTA
CLARA 128, LISBON, PORTUGAL.
WWW.SILENTLIVING.PT/HOUSES/
SANTA-CLARA-1728

View of the inner courtyard. One bedroom.
View of the bathtub from the sitting room.
Sitting room with central sofa.

Santa Clara 1728

LISBON, PORTUGAL

Created by the hotelier João Rodrigues and his family, Santa Clara 1728 is more than a guesthouse. It is a home away from home. The guesthouse is situated on one of the most romantic squares in Lisbon, in the traditionally colorful and iconic quarter of Alfama. It combines traditional Portuguese values with modern design, rooted in 18th-century history.

The renovation measures under the auspices of the architect Manuel Aires Mateus combined traditional materials such as Lioz marble with contemporary amenities. Guests are welcomed by the peaceful atmosphere, the smooth walls and hand-crafted furniture. The building opens up towards its dining room with a purpose-built oak table for 20 people, and a garden offering space for quieter moments, either relaxing or reading. The Santa Clara and Tejo suites provide luxurious accommodation with a view of the river and modern facilities. The interior is lovingly and meticulously conceived, supplemented with high-quality designer fittings. The building's carefully selected lighting creates a variety of lighting atmospheres, while the generous windows allow natural light, including the shimmering reflections from the river, to fill the interior spaces.

Interior view of the entrance hall.
Sitting area in the inner courtyard. One bathroom.
View toward the dining and breakfast room.

GETTING AROUND. SANTA CLARA 1728 IS LOCATED AT THE HEART OF THE CITY, IN THE DIRECT VICINITY OF THE ALFAMA AND GRAÇA QUARTERS. THE AREA IS KNOWN FOR THE FEIRA DA LADRA, LISBON'S LEGENDARY FLEA AND ANTIQUES MARKET. MANY INTERESTING SIGHTS ARE WITHIN WALKING DISTANCE FROM SANTA CLARA 1728, INCLUDING THE 17TH-CENTURY MONASTERY OF SÃO VICENTE DE FORA, AND THE MAJESTIC NATIONAL PANTHEON. THE ENCHANTING ALFAMA NEIGHBORHOOD IS A MAZE OF NARROW STREETS, FADO, AND FAMOUS VIEWPOINTS (MIRADOUROS). THE COMMERCIAL CITY CENTER, BAIXA, IS ABOUT 15 MINUTES' WALK AWAY, OR VISITORS CAN RIDE ON ONE OF LISBON'S PICTURESQUE OLD TRAMS.

INFORMATION. ARCHITECT>
DOROTHÉE DELAYE INTERIOR
DESIGN // 1930, RENOVATION
2022. VILLA> 380 SQM //
14 GUESTS // 6 BEDROOMS //
6 BATHROOMS. ADDRESS>
AVENUE DU TOUR DU LAC 802,
HOSSEGOR, FRANCE.
WWW.ICONIC.HOUSE/
LES-BORDS-DU-LAC

Interior view of the living room with fireplace.
Interior of one bathroom. View of the covered
poolside lounge area.

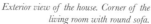

Exterior view of the house. Corner of the living room with round sofa.

Les Bords du Lac

HOSSEGOR, FRANCE

Les Bords du Lac is Iconic House's take on the ultimate ocean house: a magnificent holiday home, just a stone's throw from the Atlantic's incredible waves. It owes its ambitious décor to the interior architect, who made bold material and color choices. The house boasts a vibrant interior, combining antique furniture, custom pieces, and works of art for a stylish and sun-drenched feel that is resolutely Californian. The property surprises, astonishes, and amazes. It boasts a truly singular style.

The building accommodates seven comfortable bedrooms, each with an en-suite bathroom and a unique design, featuring plenty of curiosities. Two separate buildings house four rooms: three double rooms and one children's room in the main house, plus three double rooms in the small house, La Conciergerie. A local artist painted the mural in the pool house. Her compositions create a dreamy and geometrical interplay of colors, shapes and textures.

Interior view of the dining area. Kitchen with central cooking island. One bedroom. View of the house façade.

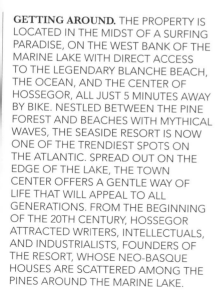

GETTING AROUND. THE PROPERTY IS LOCATED IN THE MIDST OF A SURFING PARADISE, ON THE WEST BANK OF THE MARINE LAKE WITH DIRECT ACCESS TO THE LEGENDARY BLANCHE BEACH, THE OCEAN, AND THE CENTER OF HOSSEGOR, ALL JUST 5 MINUTES AWAY BY BIKE. NESTLED BETWEEN THE PINE FOREST AND BEACHES WITH MYTHICAL WAVES, THE SEASIDE RESORT IS NOW ONE OF THE TRENDIEST SPOTS ON THE ATLANTIC. SPREAD OUT ON THE EDGE OF THE LAKE, THE TOWN CENTER OFFERS A GENTLE WAY OF LIFE THAT WILL APPEAL TO ALL GENERATIONS. FROM THE BEGINNING OF THE 20TH CENTURY, HOSSEGOR ATTRACTED WRITERS, INTELLECTUALS, AND INDUSTRIALISTS, FOUNDERS OF THE RESORT, WHOSE NEO-BASQUE HOUSES ARE SCATTERED AMONG THE PINES AROUND THE MARINE LAKE.

INFORMATION. ARCHITECT>
PEDRO FERREIRA PINTO // 2011.
HOUSE> 300 SQM // 6 GUESTS //
3 BEDROOMS // 3 BATHROOMS.
ADDRESS> PEGO BEACH,
COMPORTA, PORTUGAL.
WWW.CASADOPEGO.COM

*View of the patio from the dining area. Interior view
of the kitchen. View of Casa do Pego from above.*

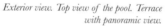
Exterior view. Top view of the pool. Terrace with panoramic view.

Casa do Pego

COMPORTA, PORTUGAL

Casa do Pego is a special retreat where nature meets architecture and great design, only a five-minute walk from the beach. The exquisite, clean design smoothly blends concrete, glass windows, and pine wood decks. Filled with iconic mid-century modern classics, Casa do Pego is the never-ending "art project" of a Lisbon-based family.

The suspended fireplace and heated floors make it irresistible throughout the year, ideal for off-season breaks. This fully equipped home has three bedrooms, accommodates six people, and is just one hour away from Lisbon and its International Airport. The roof features a sunny terrace and a wonderful heated swimming pool. The spacious terrace has an elevated position to ensure maximum privacy.

Covered in pine wood, it is ideal for sunbathing and relaxing, as well as watching the sunset while hearing the sound of the ocean, facing the green fields, and enjoying the view of Arrabida Mountain. The pool's controlled temperature allows swimming at night under the starry Comporta sky.

Main view of the house from the beach. Living room with suspended fireplace.

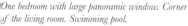

One bedroom with large panoramic window. Corner of the living room. Swimming pool.

GETTING AROUND. CASA DO PEGO IS JUST A FEW METERS AWAY FROM THE BEACH. THE NEARBY CARVALHAL BEACH, COMPORTA BEACH, ABERTA NOVA BEACH, AND MANY WILD, DESERTED SPOTS ARE WORTH EXPLORING. THE COMPORTA BEACH AREA IS BASICALLY A SINGLE, CONTINUOUS SAND LINE EXTENDING FOR MORE THAN 40 KILOMETERS FROM TROIA TO SINES. COMPORTA IS A MAGICAL PLACE, EXPLODING WITH WILDLIFE ALL YEAR AROUND. IT IS THE PERFECT SPOT FOR ANYONE WHO LOVES NATURE AND OUTDOOR ACTIVITIES, SUCH AS SAILING, SURFING, FISHING, CYCLING, BIRDWATCHING, DOLPHIN-WATCHING, AND HORSE RIDING ON THE BEACH. THE EXCELLENT RESTAURANTS ARE ALSO ONE OF THE GREATEST HIGHLIGHTS OF THIS AMAZING AREA.

INFORMATION. ARCHITECTS>
EVELYN ALONSO RONHER AND
JOSÉ ANTONIO SOSA // 2014.
EMBLEMATIC HOUSE > 114 SQM //
6 GUESTS // 3 BEDROOMS //
4 BATHROOMS. ADDRESS> C.
TORRES 17, TRIANA, LAS PALMAS
DE GRAN CANARIA, SPAIN.
WWW.THELOFTLASPALMAS.COM

The Loft

GRAN CANARIA, SPAIN

The architects converted a 19th-century town house in the historical shopping district of Triana and designed apartments that immediately give its guests a feeling of visiting friends. The apartments are family-owned and managed by the architects themselves. The inviting staircase impresses with its dark steps, lathed banisters, white-plastered structure, and the blue sky visible through the skylight. In the apartments, the floor is covered with wood and tiles, giving the spaces an urban, individual flair. The combination of white walls, old, restored French windows, and interleaved floors creates exciting spatial configurations.

A 50 square meters flat on the ground floor is designed as a split-level loft, mattresses are simply placed on the wooden sleeping platform, which is separated from the living areas and yet not concealed. Mirrors and light create transparency. The apartments on the upper floor, also 50 square meters, are laid out with an open-plan living and sleeping area. The furnishing is a cheerful, well-balanced mix of vintage and contemporary design. The sun patio also offers several levels. On the lowest platform you can sunbathe in complete privacy, while a few steps higher up, you can enjoy the rooftop townscape of the old town.

The rooftop terrace with a view of the city. Access to the terrace. New and existing stairs from below. Interior view of one room.

View of the stairwell from above. Exterior view from the street. Ground floor plan and typical floor plan. Interior view.

GETTING AROUND. THE TRIANAS NEIGHBORHOOD IS RENOWNED FOR ITS CHARMING STREETS, DIVERSE ARRAY OF SHOPS, AND CULINARY DELIGHTS. THE NEIGHBORHOOD'S CHARM LIES IN ITS PRESERVATION OF QUAINT TRADITIONAL ESTABLISHMENTS SUCH AS HABERDASHERIES, BAKERIES, ICE CREAM PARLORS, SHOE SHOPS, AND FASHION BOUTIQUES, COEXISTING SEAMLESSLY WITH CONTEMPORARY DESIGN AND FASHION TRENDS. TRIANA ALSO BOASTS SOME OF THE FINEST RESTAURANTS IN GRAN CANARIA. CONVENIENTLY LOCATED JUST A SHORT STROLL FROM THE HISTORICAL VEGUETA NEIGHBORHOOD, IT IS A GOOD OPPORTUNITY TO EXPLORE ONE OF THE MOST PICTURESQUE DISTRICTS IN LAS PALMAS DE GRAN CANARIA.

INFORMATION. ARCHITECT>
STUDIO ARTE – ARCHITECTURE
AND DESIGN // 2016.
HOUSE> 180 SQM // 6 GUESTS //
3 BEDROOMS // 3 BATHROOMS.
ADDRESS> RUA NOVA DA BOA
VISTA 49, SILVES, PORTUGAL.
WWW.CASADALILASILVES.COM

Dinig and living area with fireplace. Interior view.
View of kitchen with balcony.

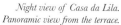
Night view of Casa da Lila.
Panoramic view from the terrace.

Casa da Lila

SILVES, PORTUGAL

Nestled in the heart of Silves, Portugal, Casa da Lila has been comprehensively renovated, experiencing a remarkable transformation. The house's initial condition was a challenge, since it was a completely dilapidated ruin. The architectural practice Studio Arte, in collaboration with the owners, transformed the decaying ruin into innovatively designed and enchanting accommodation. What at first appears to be a small single-story house, turns out to be a spacious three-level home offering spectacular views across the city of Silves and the surrounding hills.

The ground floor consists of a bedroom and en-suite bathroom, a living room with a wood burner, and a kitchen with a patio. Downstairs on the garden level, another spacious bedroom includes a bathroom with a rain shower.

The garden, complete with wooden decking, is equipped with a plunge pool (3.80 x 2.00 meters) and an outdoor shower. The comfortable master bedroom, with an open bathroom including a free-standing tub, a rain shower, and a separate toilet, is located on the top level. The master bedroom has direct access to a terrace with a lounge sofa, an outdoor shower and an outdoor kitchen.

Casa da Lila is officially registered for holiday rentals in the city of Silves.

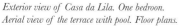

Exterior view of Casa da Lila. One bedroon.
Aerial view of the terrace with pool. Floor plans.

GETTING AROUND. SILVES, A HISTORICAL CITY LOCATED IN SOUTHERN PORTUGAL, WAS THE CAPITAL OF THE ALGARVE DURING ITS MOORISH OCCUPATION. ITS HISTORICAL SIGNIFICANCE IS EVIDENT IN ITS WELL-PRESERVED ARCHITECTURE, INCLUDING THE IMPRESSIVE SILVES CASTLE, WHICH STANDS AS A SYMBOL OF ITS MEDIEVAL PAST. SILVES HOSTS VARIOUS CULTURAL EVENTS THROUGHOUT THE YEAR, ATTRACTING BOTH LOCALS AND TOURISTS. THE MEDIEVAL FAIR IS A POPULAR EVENT HELD WITHIN THE GROUNDS OF THE CASTLE. THE CITY IS LOCATED NEAR SOME OF THE MOST PRESTIGIOUS GOLF COURSES IN THE ALGARVE, 25 MINUTES FROM THE NEAREST BEACH AND 45 MINUTES FROM THE NEAREST AIRPORT.

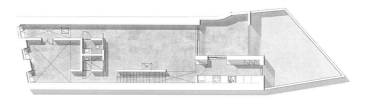

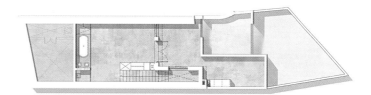

INFORMATION. ARCHITECTS>
LIZ & CORENTIN LAMOUR // 2002.
HAMLET OF 9 COUNTRY COTTAGES>
2–6 GUESTS PER COTTAGE.
ADDRESS> LE MOURVET NOIR 4,
PLÉLO, BRETAGNE, FRANCE.
WWW.INTOTHEPRAIRIE.COM

Into the Prairie

The Prairie Cottages are situated in the heart of a working farm, surrounded by prairies and a small wood, where the cows graze. Each house has a private garden with a view of the meadows. All nine unique, very private houses and barns, as well as the farmhouse, have been carefully restored, focusing on sustainability and the use of natural materials, thereby transforming the stone houses into warm, inviting accommodation for self-sufficient visitors.

Earthy tones, organic structures and maritime accentuation express a relaxed atmosphere and timeless refinement. Each holiday home has its own style, fitted with vintage gems, creative upcycling projects and comfortable beds and furniture. Six of the houses have wood fires that ensure a cozy ambiance during in the autumn and winter. Optional breakfast baskets are available with freshly baked scones, regional cakes, homemade juice, and marmelade from the orchard. Anyone wishing to cook in the well-equipped kitchen is welcome to use the farm's vegetable garden and greenhouse, offering herbs, lettuce varieties, and even edible flowers.

Exterior view of the glasshouse. Isidore double-height living room with dining area. Joséphine garden view. Exterior view of the Rose cottage.

Isidore dining area with large window overlooking the Louise cottage. Anna round bathroom. View of Isidore barn from the garden.

GETTING AROUND. THE NEAREST VILLAGE OFFERINGS SHOPS, SMALL CAFÉS, AND RESTAURANTS IS ONLY A FEW MINUTES' WALK AWAY. THE SEA IS AROUND TEN MINUTES AWAY BY CAR, WITH A CHOICE OF 20 DIFFERENT BEACHES ALONG THE COAST. THE CÔTES-D'ARMOR OFFERS A SERIES OF PICTURESQUE DESTINATIONS. DISCOVER THE FLORAL PARADISE OF THE CAR-FREE ÎLE DE BRÉHAT. THE CHARMING HARBOR TOWN OF PAIMPOL AND THE GRANITE COAST, WITH ITS PINK-COLORED CLIFFS, ARE WORTH VISITING. NATURALLY, THE UNESCO WORLD HERITAGE SITE OF MONT SAINT-MICHEL IS A MUST.

INFORMATION. ARCHITECTS>
PABLO PITA ARQUITECTOS, HEIM
BALP ARCHITEKTEN, BACANA
STUDIO // 2020. APARTHOTEL>
2,700 SQM // 40 APARTMENTS.
ADDRESS> RUA DO BONJARDIM
541, PORTO, PORTUGAL.
WWW.VILLAGEBYBOA.COM

*Interior view of The Space, Village by BOA's
penthouse conceived for private events. Cozy corner on
the balcony. View of the common terrace with garden.*

Interior view of a large living room. One kitchen.

Village by BOA

PORTO, PORTUGAL

The first BOA Hotels project is an ode to fully exploring the space and memory of the "Bairro do Silva", a historical neighborhood in the heart of Porto. Pablo Pita Arquitectos, in partnership with Heim Balp Architekten, were responsible for modernizing the buildings.

With the interior design predominantly the work of Bacana Studio, BOA Hotels group has created an experience which reproduces the feeling of being at home – with hotel service, and based on four key pillars: aesthetics, comfort, world-class service and cutting-edge technology.

Village by BOA features a fitness center, an elegantly designed penthouse for events, and a boutique deli market. The complex is fitted with smart locks, ensuring privacy and convenience for its guests.

In Village by BOA, the historical richness of the "Bairro do Silva" seamlessly merges with the innovation of modern hospitality, creating a destination that both honors Porto's heritage and embodies contemporary elegance and comfort.

Exterior view of the apartments from the garden. The inner courtyard precedes the apartments and invites guests to relax. One bedroom. View of the spiral staircase.

GETTING AROUND. VILLAGE BY BOA IS LOCATED IN THE HEART OF PORTO, IN THE ICONIC BOLHÃO MARKET QUARTER, NEAR TRINDADE METRO STATION AND THE CITY'S MAIN BOULEVARD, AVENIDA DOS ALIADOS. THE QUARTER OFFERS NEARBY DELI-STORES, HISTORICAL SHOPS AND RENOWNED RESTAURANTS SERVING THE BEST FOOD IN THE CITY. WHILE IN PORTO, TAKE THE TIME TO VISIT SÃO BENTO STATION, THE CLÉRIGOS TOWER, AND MIGUEL BOMBARDA CREATIVE QUARTER.

INFORMATION. ARCHITECT>
MECANISMO // 2017. HOTEL>
10,000 SQM // 44 GUESTS //
22 BEDROOMS // 22 BATHROOMS.
ADDRESS> PADRE ORKOLAGA
IBILBIDEA 56, SAN SEBASTIÁN, SPAIN.
WWW.AKELARRE.NET

*View of the common lounge
with fireplace. Main staircase.*

Akelarre
Hotel

SAN SEBASTIÁN, SPAIN

The Akelarre Hotel is the result of over forty years of identity and development. It represents the fusion of tradition and time with a dedication to research and innovation. It is precisely the symbiosis of integrating context and innovation that defines the spirit of the hotel.

Situated just a few kilometers from the center of San Sebastián, on the northern slope of Mount Igueldo, overlooking the Cantabrian Sea, the hotel consists of five stone cubicles emerging from the mountainside towards the sea, housing twenty-two rooms within.

Attention to detail and sustainable design are the distinguishing features of the hotel, highlighted by the use of locally sourced natural materials that seamlessly blend it into its surroundings and create a warm welcome throughout its spacious interiors.

Exterior view of the hotel overlooking the ocean.
Interior view of the common area..

GETTING AROUND. LOOKING OUT TO SEA, THE BAY WINDOWS AND TERRACES OFFER STUNNING VIEWS OF THE BASQUE FRENCH COASTLINE, ORIO AND GETARIA HARBORS, AND THE BISCAY COASTAL CLIFFS. THE BREATHTAKING SCENERY INVITES VISITORS TO RELAX, SURROUNDED BY NATURE. THE PROXIMITY TO THE CITY CENTER ALLOWS THEM TO ENJOY THE MYRIAD CHARMS OF SAN SEBASTIAN, ONE OF THE JEWELS OF THE CANTABRIAN COAST, DUE TO ITS INNOVATIVE CUISINE, THE BEAUTY OF ITS BEACHES, THE QUALITY AND DIVERSITY OF ITS SHOPPING, AND ITS WIDE RANGE OF CULTURAL OFFERS.

Interior view of one room.
Axonometric view. Wellness area.

Swimming pool with panoramic views.
Interior view of the relax area. View of the
lounge area on the terrace.

INFORMATION. ARCHITECT>
ATELIER RUA // 2015.
HOUSE> 285 SQM // 12 GUESTS //
6 BEDROOMS // 7 BATHROOMS.
ADDRESS> CATIVA, TAVIRA,
PORTUGAL.
WWW.PENSAOAGRICOLA.COM

One bedroom with en suite bathroom.
Exterior view of the terrace with stone benches.
View of the dining room.

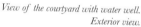
View of the courtyard with water well.
Exterior view.

Pensão Agricola

TAVIRA, PORTUGAL

Located near the city of Tavira, between the Algarve mountain range to the north and the Ria Formosa nature reserve to the south, Pensão Agricola is situated in a rural area dominated by agriculture. The elongated plot is divided into two zones accommodating the main building and several auxiliary buildings. One enters the property from the north via an attractive avenue of olive and carob trees. The south includes a more private, secluded area dominated by a beautiful orchard.

The main building was renovated using traditional building methods, thereby preserving the original character and charm of the ensemble. The house's social and functional areas are situated there: the reception, kitchen, three small combined lounges and kitchens, and two bedrooms. The ceilings are clad in white-painted reeds, while the floor is consistently covered by a smooth screed. Around the main building, three new volumes are connected by walls of varying thicknesses and heights. The walls define relaxing areas that are connected to the main building to form individual patios for the new rooms.

Interior view of the living room. Terrace with swimming pool. Exterior view of different buildings. Outdoor seating area. Floor plan.

GETTING AROUND. TAVIRA IS A CITY BRIMMING WITH HISTORY AND NATURAL SPLENDOR. ITS ROMAN BRIDGE SPANS THE GILÃO RIVER, OFFERING VISTAS OF THE OLD TOWN'S WHITEWASHED BUILDINGS AND NARROW STREETS. THE NEARBY RIA FORMOSA NATURE RESERVE IS TEEMING WITH WILDLIFE. VISITORS TO THIS COASTAL PARADISE CAN ENJOY THE SCENERY ON WALKS THROUGH THE SALT MARSHES AND DUNES, AS WELL AS THE UNTOUCHED BEACHES. ONLY A FEW KILOMETERS AWAY, THE PICTURESQUE VILLAGE OF CACELA VELHA IS PERCHED UPON THE CLIFF. THE BREATHTAKING VIEWS, THE EXQUISITE OYSTERS AND FANTASTIC SUNSETS ARE ALL EXCEPTIONAL.

INFORMATION. ARCHITECT>
ATELIER JQTS // 2021. HOUSE>
170 SQM // 4 GUESTS // 3 BEDROOMS
// 3 BATHROOMS. ADDRESS>
PRACETA ENGENHEIRO MANUEL
MENEZES 83, ALCABIDECHE,
CASCAIS, PORTUGAL.
WWW.BOUTIQUE-HOMES.COM/
VACATION-RENTALS/EUROPE/
PORTUGAL/UNTITLED-HOUSE

UNTITLED
House

CASCAIS, PORTUGAL

Untitled is a single-family home on a single floor. The reinforced concrete structure consists of large-scale beams in longitudinal and transverse directions, which define the organization of the rooms. Each room is characterized by a series of secondary beams that define the character through their smaller dimensions. The striking roof and ceiling plate form the spatial and functional components of the special building and define its architectural character.

The design only uses a small number of different elements, thereby strengthening its expressive quality. All rectangular windows have the same size. Only their changing arrangement reflects the uses behind them and establishes a relationship with the outdoor environment. The materials exist in a mutual dialogue. The coarse concrete appears in its original condition, while the wood retains its natural color and texture, both for the interior furniture and in the frames of the apertures. Pigmented lime with a reddish color and a smooth surface was used for the exterior walls. Its tone varies depending on the light incidence, contrasting with the coarse, structured concrete.

Exterior view of UNTITLED House.
Interior view of the living room. Kitchen area.
Main view from the street.

Interior view of one bedroom. Detail of the exterior façade with window. Floor plan. Exterior view.

GETTING AROUND. CASCAIS IS SITUATED WEST OF LISBON AND IS FAMOUS FOR ITS BEAUTIFUL BEACHES, BEACH ACTIVITIES, MAGNIFICENT COASTAL LANDSCAPE, YACHT HARBOR AND CULTURAL HERITAGE, SUCH AS THE MEDIEVAL NOSSA SENHORA FORTRESS AND THE FORMER ROYAL SUMMER RESIDENCE. IT IS A GOOD STARTING POINT FOR EXCURSIONS TO TOWNS AND THE NEARBY REGION.

INFORMATION. ARCHITECT>
ART HERITAGE HANS FALK, PROJECT
BY KONSTANTIN FALK // 2016.
FARMHOUSE> 600 SQM // 12 GUESTS
// 5 BEDROOMS // 5 BATHROOMS.
ADDRESS> ROUTE DE LA MALBRECHE
424, LIEU-DIT LES ROCHERS, CERISY LA
FORÊT, BASSE-NORMANDIE, FRANCE.
WWW.LESROCHERS.ONLINE

*Exterior stone walls of Les Rochers. Dining area
with large still life painting. One bedroom. Aerial view
of the manor farm.*

Les Rochers

CERISY-LA-FORÊT, FRANCE

Fortified and arranged around a once enclosed courtyard, this monumental manor farm built in the 16th century has undergone 10 years of extensive renovation by its owners while retaining its original appearance.

The outbuildings and former chapel have been converted into four spacious, independent accommodation units and an apartment. To retain the monumental size of the rooms, screening walls separate the bathrooms from the bedrooms.

An old stable was converted into a communal lounge. A huge still life separates the lounge and dining room from a beautiful semi-professional kitchen, which is available to guests.

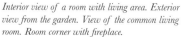

Interior view of a room with living area. Exterior view from the garden. View of the common living room. Room corner with fireplace.

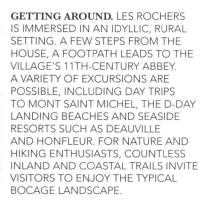

GETTING AROUND. LES ROCHERS IS IMMERSED IN AN IDYLLIC, RURAL SETTING. A FEW STEPS FROM THE HOUSE, A FOOTPATH LEADS TO THE VILLAGE'S 11TH-CENTURY ABBEY. A VARIETY OF EXCURSIONS ARE POSSIBLE, INCLUDING DAY TRIPS TO MONT SAINT MICHEL, THE D-DAY LANDING BEACHES AND SEASIDE RESORTS SUCH AS DEAUVILLE AND HONFLEUR. FOR NATURE AND HIKING ENTHUSIASTS, COUNTLESS INLAND AND COASTAL TRAILS INVITE VISITORS TO ENJOY THE TYPICAL BOCAGE LANDSCAPE.

INFORMATION. ARCHITECT>
TABAIBO ATELIER // 2020.
HOUSE> 90 SQM // 4 GUESTS //
2 BEDROOMS // 1.5 BATHROOMS.
ADDRESS> CAMINHO FAJA DO
MAR 14 A, ARCO DA CALHETA,
MADEIRA, PORTUGAL.
WWW.BANANAHOUSE.PT

*Interior view of dining and living area. Panoramic
view of the Atlantic Ocean. The pool terrace of the
Banana House.*

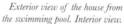
Exterior view of the house from the swimming pool. Interior view.

The Banana House

MADEIRA, PORTUGAL

Relax among the mango, fig and banana trees in a luxury private paradise. The Banana House is located between the stunning mountains and thousands of banana trees in a hidden piece of heaven on Madeira Island. The unique designer house offers peace, privacy, relaxation, and laid-back luxury comfort. Visitors can refresh in the private and spacious saltwater pool.

Alternatively, they can simply enjoy the sun, do some Yoga on the pool patio or lose themselves on the cozy sunbed while watching the waves of the ocean. And for those who want to combine the pleasant with the useful, a desk and high-speed Internet are provided – workation at its best.

The most magical moment of the day can be experienced on the spacious barbecue terrace, when the sun sinks into the Atlantic Ocean and the banana leaves rustle in the gentle wind – simply breathtaking.

*The house surrounded by banana trees.
View of one bedroom. The terrace overlooking
the ocean at sunset.*

GETTING AROUND. IN THIS
HIDDEN PARADISE FOR DESIGN
LOVERS, ADVENTURERS, AND
CONNOISSEURS, VISITORS
CAN DO YOGA EXERCISES ON
THE POOL PATIO, HAVE A SWIM
IN THE ATLANTIC OCEAN - JUST
A FEW MINUTES WALK FROM
THE HOUSE - OR EXPLORE
THE BEAUTIFUL COUNTRYSIDE
BY BIKE OR ON FOOT. THE
BANANA HOUSE IS A PERFECT
BASE ON THE ISLAND.

INFORMATION. ARCHITECT>
GONZALO GARCIA. DESIGNER>
LUIS SANTULLANO // 2009.
SUITE > 90 SQM // 4 GUESTS //
2 BEDROOMS // 2 BATHROOMS.
ADDRESS> VILLADEMOROS,
VALDES, ASTURIAS, SPAIN.
WWW.TORREVILLADEMOROS.COM

Exterior view of the entrance to the tower.
Panoramic view from the suite.

Torre de Villademoros

VALDES, SPAIN

Hotel Torre de Villademoros was created out of an 18th-century manor house. Situated on the same property, the stately tower that gives the hotel its name is undoubtedly one of the best examples of medieval military architecture in Asturias.

The tower has been restored to house a suite that retains the original masonry walls, since they were in an acceptable state of conservation. The interior has a contemporary character, with stairs and interior walls in chestnut, the most widely used wood in the area's traditional architecture.

The top level features a roof terrace, as well as windows that help illuminate the interior. From this watchtower, one can enjoy incredible views of the coastal area, the mountains, and the marine horizon.

View of one bedroom with wooden staircase. Interior views of the living room.

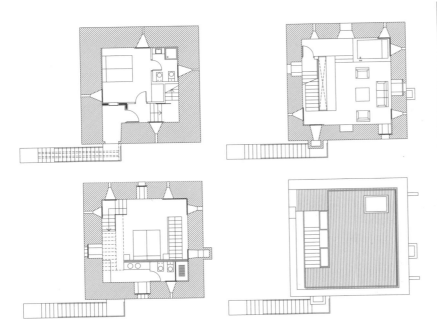

TORRE DE VILLADEMOROS IS AN EXCELLENT STARTING POINT TO DISCOVER THE WESTERN COAST OF ASTURIAS, ONE OF THE BEST PRESERVED COASTAL STRETCHES OF THE IBERIAN PENINSULA. FROM THE TOWER, YOU CAN WALK TO IMPOSING CLIFFS AND WILD COVES. SOME OF THE MOST BEAUTIFUL FISHING PORTS IN THE REGION ARE WITHIN A 20-MINUTE DRIVE. TOWARD THE INTERIOR, SMALL VILLAGES, VALLEYS, AND RIVERS ARE LOCATED IN AREAS BARELY AFFECTED BY TOURISM.

View of the tower surrounded by greenery. Floor plans. Bathroom.

Interior view of the master bedroom. Tower rooftop terrace. Exterior view of the covered terrace connected with the dining area.

INFORMATION. ARCHITECT>
STUDIODOIS // 2019. HOUSES>
181 SQM // 6 GUESTS //
3 BEDROOMS // 2 BATHROOMS.
ADDRESS> CAMINHO LEVADA
DA VARGEM 9, PONTA DO SOL,
MADEIRA, PORTUGAL.
WWW.CASASDAVARGEM.COM

*View of the kitchen and dining area with large
panoramic window. Exterior detail of a corner
window. View of the infinity pool.*

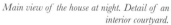
Main view of the house at night. Detail of an interior courtyard.

Casas da Vargem

MADEIRA, PORTUGAL

Nestled in Ponda do Sol's valley, Madeira, this project harmoniously integrates two semi-detached holiday homes inspired by the scale of the traditional stone storage building. The structures cascade down the sloping terrain, forming patios and gardens.

Viewed from across the valley, the building appears as a collection of smaller volumes, blending seamlessly with the surroundings. Internally, the rooms follow the natural slope, connecting directly to gardens and patios, each offering varying levels of privacy, solar exposure, and shade. A shared pool, surrounded by lush vegetation, ensures maximum privacy, complemented by private exterior bathtubs for each house.

Traditional materials, such as wooden floors, exposed stone façades, and "calçada portuguesa" terraces, pay homage to local craftsmanship.

Exterior view of Casas da Vargem. Living room with large corner sofa. Swimming pool from above. Floor plan.

GETTING AROUND. LOMBADA, PONTA DO SOL OFFERS TRAILS THAT ARE IDEAL FOR THOSE WHO WANT TO EXPLORE THE TRADITIONAL LEVADAS OF MADEIRA ISLAND. LOCATED ON THE SOUTHWEST COAST, THE ROUTES ARE DEFINED BY THE MOUNTAINOUS AND OCEANIC LANDSCAPE. THE AREA IS RURAL, BUT ALSO VERY CLOSE TO THE VILLAGE CENTER, PROVIDING BARS, RESTAURANTS, A BEACH, AND SOME TYPICAL GROCERY STORES.

INFORMATION. ARCHITECT>
DGA ARCHITECTE // 2011.
HOUSE> 150 SQM // 6 GUESTS //
2 BEDROOMS // 1 BATHROOMS.
ADDRESS> LA ROCHEBLIN,
LA GAUBRETIÈRE, FRANCE.
WWW.CHALET-CONCEPT.COM

Chalet Concept

LA GAUBRETIÈRE, FRANCE

The house is the oldest in the village of La Rocheblin, it was built with stones from the quarry that existed in the 16th century, and offers wonderful views on the surrounding countryside

Before its renovation, the ruin had no roof and only some of the walls were stable. The owners have created an oasis of recreation, with all the modern amenities required, while embedding the house in the surroundings and retaining the dimensions and appearance of the original.

View of the kitchen and dining area. Living room with mezzanine. View of the terrace accessible from the dining room. Exterior view from the garden.

View of the master bedroom with bathtub. Exterior side view from the garden. First floor plan.

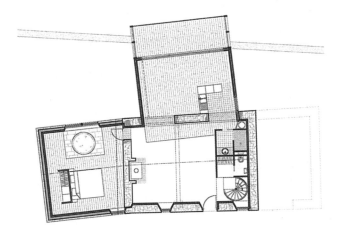

GETTING AROUND. LA ROCHELLE AND NANTES, WITH THEIR MUSEUMS AND FASCINATING HISTORY, ARE ABOUT AN HOUR AWAY. THE MORE IMMEDIATE SURROUNDINGS OFFER A VARIETY OF WINERIES, PRODUCING MUSCADET AND THE VIN DE TOURAINE, BEACH WALKS AROUND LES SABLES D'OLONNES AND PORNIC, AND HIKES AROUND THE REGION OF LA SEVRE NANTAISE.

Main view of Chalet Concept. View of the bedroom on the mezzanine with large window to the living room.

INFORMATION. ARCHITECTS>
RAUL LINO AND OUTPOST //
2018. HOUSE> 650 SQM //
18 GUESTS // 7 APARMENTS,
9 BEDROOMS // 8 BATHROOMS.
ADDRESS> AZENHAS DO MAR,
SINTRA, PORTUGAL.
WWW.OUTPOST.PT

Exterior view of the Pool House from the terrace.
Outdoor hub with panoramic view.

OUTPOST –
Casa
das Arribas

SINTRA, PORTUGAL

Casa das Arribas stands proudly on the cliffs just outside the village of Azenhas do Mar overlooking the coast from Cabo de Roca to Ericeira. It was built in the 1940s as a family estate by the enowned Portuguese architect Raul Lino.

OUTPOST carefully renovated the buildings, upgrading them to standards of modern comfort. Seven different apartments were created, combining luxury-hotel amenities with the privacy, space, and independence of one's own holiday home.

Guests share the vast garden, pool, tennis court, sauna, ice and hot tub, and a newly built yoga studio. Casa das Arribas appears to be isolated on the cliffs, offering breathtaking views of the scenery.

Interior view of a large bedroom.
Cozy corner in the living room.

GETTING AROUND. THE CASA DAS ARRIBAS PROPERTY IS LOCATED NEAR THE ICONIC CLIFF VILLAGE OF AZENHAS DO MAR, 40 KM FROM LISBON. SEVERAL BEACHES ARE WITHIN REACH, INCLUDING THE "HOME BEACH" A 5-MINUTE WALK AWAY. VARIOUS FACILITIES FOR SURFING AND ALL KINDS OF WATER SPORTS ARE AVAILABLE WITHIN 45 MINUTES' DISTANCE.

Exterior view of Casa das Arribas. Floor plan of the Ocean Saloon and the Pool House. Yoga studio with panoramic view.

Kitchen and living area with fireplace. Pool terrace with view. One bedroom.

INFORMATION. ARCHITECT>
DIEGO MERCHÁN JIMÉNEZ-
ANDRADES // 2015. HOUSE>
437 SQM // 13 GUESTS //
7 BEDROOMS // 8 BATHROOMS.
ADDRESS> EDUARDO SHELLY 6,
VEJER DE LA FRONTERA,
ANDALUSIA, SPAIN.
WWW.CASASHELLY.COM

Living area with fireplace. Inner courtyard.
Interior view of one bedroom.
View of the main courtyard of the villa.

Casa Shelly Hospedería

VEJER DE LA FRONTERA,
SPAIN

Located within the medieval walls of Vejer de la Frontera in the province of Cádiz, Casa Shelly recalls the placid life of a 19th-century home in the provinces, bathed in the bright sunlight and cooled by the fresh Atlantic breezes of the Costa de la Luz.

Casa Shelly is a place to relax, disconnect, and luxuriate in the pleasures that are offered by the land, the sea, and sunny skies of Cádiz in southern Andalusia.
The property that now houses Casa Shelly was purchased in a derelict state by the current owners in 2012.

After a restoration process that applied traditional building methods, its doors opened to receive its first guests in the summer of 2015.

Interior view of one bedroom.
Exterior view from one terrace.

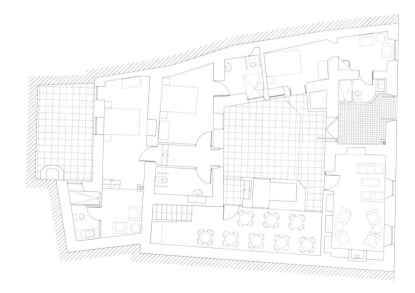

Interior view of the main courtyard.
Interior details. View of the main entrance.
Floor plan.

GETTING AROUND. VEJER OFFERS A UNIQUE BLEND OF HISTORY, CULTURE, GASTRONOMY, AND NATURE, WITH ITS WINDING COBBLESTONE STREETS, MEDIEVAL ARCHITECTURE, AND WHITEWASHED HOUSES THAT GIVE IT ITS DISTINCTIVE ANDALUSIAN CHARM. VISITORS CAN EXPLORE THE HISTORICAL CASTLE, VISIT ART GALLERIES AND CRAFT SHOPS, OR SIMPLY ENJOY ONE OF THE MANY RESTAURANTS AND CAFÉS OFFERING REGIONAL FARE. THE SURROUNDING AREA BOASTS STUNNING BEACHES, NATURAL PARKS, AND PICTURESQUE VILLAGES. WHETHER YOU ARE INTERESTED IN HISTORY, CULTURE, OR OUTDOOR ACTIVITIES, VEJER DE LA FRONTERA AND ITS SURROUNDINGS OFFER SOMETHING FOR EVERYONE.

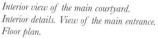

INFORMATION. ARCHITECT>
JOSÉ ADRIÃO ARQUITETOS //
19TH CENTURY, RENOVATION 2020.
13 APARTMENTS> 1,309 SQM //
44 GUESTS. ADDRESS>
RUA DOS DOURADORES 192,
BAIXA, LISBON, PORTUGAL.
WWW.ANTIGACASAPESSOA.COM

*Interior view. Main view of the
building from the street. The living area
overlooking one bedroom.*

Antiga Casa Pessoa

LISBON, PORTUGAL

The Antiga Casa Pessoa was constructed in the early 19th century, at the heart of Lisbon's Baixa Pombalina district. By 2016, the building was almost completely vacant and severely dilapidated. To make the most of the building's corner situation, it was proposed to change its configuration from two apartments to three per floor.

To address modern demands for comfort and accessibility, a lift was installed at the center of the building, leaving the original stairwell intact. Examination of the building fabric revealed the existence of successive layers of frescoes and tempera paintings in all the apartments. Preserving them was deemed one of the most important concerns of the whole project. Thus, the building task focused on preserving this heritage, adapting all technical and design decisions accordingly. Today, the traces of the past, incomplete as they were and with all their flaws, are visible to tell their own inspirational story.

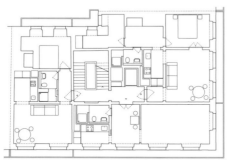

GETTING AROUND. SITUATED ON THE TEJO RIVER, THE LIVELY, CHARISMATIC CAPITAL OF PORTUGAL ENCHANTS AN EVER-GROWING NUMBER OF TOURISTS WITH ITS MULTIFACETED, BUSY LIFE, COMBINING PROGRESS AND TRADITION. IN ADDITION TO THE NARROW STREETS OF ALFAMA OLD TOWN, THE CITY ALSO BOASTS COSMOPOLITAN SHOPPING BOULEVARDS AND A WEALTH OF CULINARY SERVICES. ONLY A FEW MINUTES AWAY FROM THE ANTIGA CASA PESSOA, ONE CAN NOT ONLY ENJOY THE WATER, BEAUTIFUL SHOPS, AND RESTAURANTS, BUT ALSO TAKE IN THE CULTURAL SIGHTS, SUCH AS LISBON CATHEDRAL, THE ARCO DA RUA AUGUSTA, AND THE CASTELO DE S. JORGE.

Interior view of one room with frescoes. Floor plans. View of the restored original frescoes.

View of the kitchen. Staircase area. One bedroom.

INFORMATION. ARCHITECTS>
COLLECTIF VOUS, STUDENTS OF
ECOLE NATIONALE SUPÉRIEURE
D'ARCHITECTURE DE NANTES //
2018–2020. CABINS> CA. 35 SQM
PER CABIN // FROM 2 TO 4 GUESTS
PER CABIN // 1 BEDROOM PER
CABIN // 1 BATHROOM PER CABIN.
ADDRESS> KERGO 19, PLOEMEL,
BRETAGNE, FRANCE.
WWW.LABELLEFOLIE.FR

*Interior view of Cabin Superpausée. Exterior view of
Cabin Keravan. View of the surrounding nature from
the bed area of Cabin Superpausée.*

Exterior view of Cabin Superpausée.
Interior view of Cabin Cactus.

La Belle Folie

PLOEMEL, FRANCE

La Belle Folie is a place dedicated to relaxation and leisure. It is different, singular, lively, and conducive to encounters, sharing, and solidarity. It also reflects a social and ecological sensibility: a place to eat well, have fun, learn, dream, and sometimes even stay awake. What is important here is that everyone feels at home, whatever their age, wherever they are from and wherever they are going.

A cabin of 35 square meters with one bedroom, a large lounge, bathroom and garden: Cabin Superpausée was inspired by an iconic popular French object, the fisherman's seat, and by the camping tent. The main characteristic of Cabin Cactus is its light. All the windows face the sky, visible through the zenith at a height of 8 meters. This creates a very peaceful atmosphere.

The house is entirely made of wood. Also completely out of wood, Cabin Branchée was inspired by tree branches. The entire structure was cut with a DCN machine by students at the School of Architecture of Nantes. The external envelope is made with chestnut wood. Cabin Keravan is perfect for a romantic getaway all year round. A non-translucent curtain closes off this warm cocoon. The menhir is equipped with a shower and toilet.

Sleeping and living area with large
windows of Cabin La Branchée.
Exterior view of Cabin La Branchée.

View of nature from the catamaran net terrace of Cabin Superpausée. View of the sleeping area with skylight windows of Cabin Cactus. Exterior view of Cabin Cactus.

GETTING AROUND. DISCOVER THE GOLFE DU MORBIHAN, THE CARNAC BEACHES AND THE MEGALITHS, AS WELL AS THE MEDIEVAL CITIES OF VANNES AND AURAY, THE VANNES JAZZ FESTIVAL, THE HARBOR AT LA TRINITÉ-SUR-MER, AND ITS RACING BOATS. THE ISLANDS BELLE-ÎLE-EN-MER, HOUAT, AND HOEDIC ARE ALL NEARBY.

INFORMATION. ARCHITECT>
PAR – PLATAFORMA DE
ARQUITECTURA // 2022.
HOUSE> 257 SQM // 6 GUESTS //
3 BEDROOMS // 3 BATHROOMS.
ADDRESS> RUA ALMEIDA
GARRETT 53, FARO, PORTUGAL.
WWW.CASA1923.PT

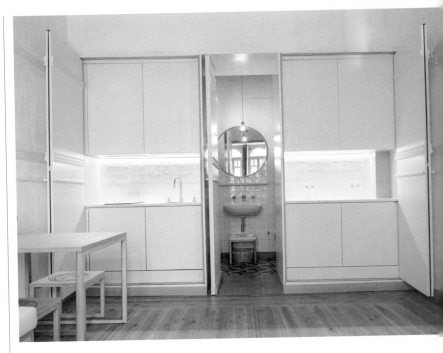

View of the inner courtyard. One bedroom.
View of the kitchen cabinet with entrance to the
bathroom. Main view of Casa 1923.

Casa 1923

FARO, PORTUGAL

Casa 1923 invites you to enter a house with history in a magical 1920s atmosphere. The project is aimed at renovating and expanding the existing building, while simultaneously restoring the exterior and interior. The architects' concept also envisages rescuing the authenticity that was almost lost, both on an architectural and a historical level, thereby contributing to sustainable development.

The ground floor accommodates the main apartment (kitchen, living, and dining rooms), along with two studios, which can be used separately or as a single unit. On the upper floor, the two accommodation units with contemporary features communicate with a central zone equipped with a kitchen and a multipurpose room.

The house is hybrid, also mirrored on the outside by the organic vegetable garden, an edible garden, a water well on the ground floor, and a pool on the upper floor, where the idyllic greenery overgrows the space and sustainability is a way of life, rather than just a concept.

The garden with external staircase. Interior view of a common room. View of the surroundings from the pool on the terrace. Axonometric view.

GETTING AROUND. THE MARINA AND VILA ADENTRO, THE HISTORICAL CENTER OF FARO, ARE JUST A FEW MINUTES AWAY. CASA 1923 IS PART OF THE MODERNIST ARCHITECTURE WALKING TOUR - A GUIDE TO THE BEST MODERN BUILDINGS IN FARO. THE CITY HAS A LARGE DIVERSITY OF ARCHITECTURAL HERITAGE, INVITING VISITORS TO EMBARK ON A VARIETY OF WALKS.

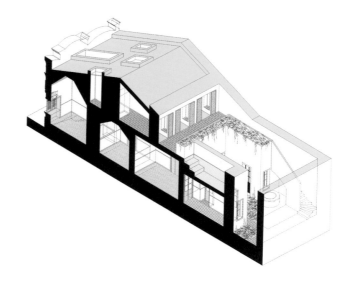

INFORMATION. ARCHITECTS>
JAMIE FOBERT ARCHITECTS AND
MARTA GUTIERREZ MOSQUERA //
2017. MAIN HOUSE AND CABANA>
170 SQM AND 40 SQM // 8 AND
4 GUESTS // 4 AND 1 BEDROOMS //
4 AND 1 BATHROOMS. ADDRESS>
DONON, CANGAS DO
MORRAZO, GALICIA, SPAIN.
WWW.CAMINODEPLAYA.COM

Aerial view of the main house and the cabana.
View from the courtyard of the corten sliding shutters.
Interior view of one bedroom.

Living room with fireplace. View of the outdoor seating area.

Camino de Playa

CANGAS DO MORRAZO, SPAIN

The Costa da Vela Nature Reserve in Galicia sits on the very edge of Europe. The untamed, sparsely inhabited land meets the wild Atlantic with long stretches of beautiful white beaches. In 2004, today's owners came across the ruins of a long-abandoned house on one of the sandy paths that wind down through the pine trees to the sea. Fascinated by their discovery, they transformed the ruin into a comfortable country refuge.

With a size of 170 square meters, the house has four bedrooms and an inner courtyard, retaining the strong walls of irregular granite blocks. An infinity pool cascades down a wall of the new inner courtyard, which provides an attractive outdoor space surrounded by pine, olive, and chestnut trees, as well as succulent plants. The interior is simply detailed, revealing the building's construction. The granite walls and chestnut ceiling are exposed. The kitchen features a vernacular barrel-vaulted ceiling. Each bedroom has its own shower and WC.

An adjacent small building has been transformed into a second little house, the Cabaña, with its own kitchen and shower. The little house is materially consistent with the main house, with exposed granite, built-in chestnut joinery, and Corten shutters, and also has its terrace and outdoor kitchen extending discreetly into the nature reserve.

Exterior view of the Camino de Playa and
the infinity pool. Outdoor dining area.

View of the kitchen and dining area. One bedroom.
Exterior view of the courtyard.

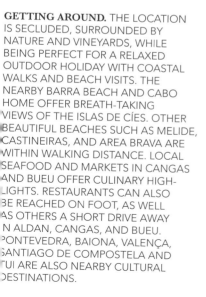

GETTING AROUND. THE LOCATION IS SECLUDED, SURROUNDED BY NATURE AND VINEYARDS, WHILE BEING PERFECT FOR A RELAXED OUTDOOR HOLIDAY WITH COASTAL WALKS AND BEACH VISITS. THE NEARBY BARRA BEACH AND CABO HOME OFFER BREATH-TAKING VIEWS OF THE ISLAS DE CÍES. OTHER BEAUTIFUL BEACHES SUCH AS MELIDE, CASTINEIRAS, AND AREA BRAVA ARE WITHIN WALKING DISTANCE. LOCAL SEAFOOD AND MARKETS IN CANGAS AND BUEU OFFER CULINARY HIGH-LIGHTS. RESTAURANTS CAN ALSO BE REACHED ON FOOT, AS WELL AS OTHERS A SHORT DRIVE AWAY IN ALDAN, CANGAS, AND BUEU. PONTEVEDRA, BAIONA, VALENÇA, SANTIAGO DE COMPOSTELA AND TUI ARE ALSO NEARBY CULTURAL DESTINATIONS.

INFORMATION. ARCHITECT> JOÃO PEDRO FALCÃO DE CAMPOS // 2021. HOUSE> 330 SQM // 7 GUESTS // 3 BEDROOMS // 4 BATHROOMS. ADDRESS> ALAMEDA DA PRAIA DO PEGO, COMPORTA, PORTUGAL. WWW.PURACOMPORTA.COM

Interior view of the large and bright dining area open to the terrace. View of the corridor. Exterior view of the house.

Pura Comporta

COMPORTA, PORTUGAL

The villa features panoramic windows all around and super-modern, minimalist interiors. To one side the large glass windows open onto a suspended decked terrace overlooking rural fields, over which you can also enjoy spectacular ocean sunsets and extended views all the way to the Serra da Arrábida coastline. To the other side, nestled between the villa and sand dunes, and framed by pine trees, lies the large, heated, and totally private swimming pool, which in turn is surrounded by a decked terrace for chilling out and outdoor dining.

The Design Villa has been conceived to welcome young families, with all interior to exterior windows/doors featuring special child-safe locks. There are three suites plus a mezzanine level for an extra guest. From the bathtub of the master bedroom suite, you can also enjoy those wonderful sunsets. The dining room opens both ways, to the pool's decked area and to the covered terrace. Stylish designer furniture and atmospheric lights create a unique mood. Equipped with central heating, air conditioning, and ceiling ventilators in the bedrooms, as well as floor-heating in the bathrooms, the villa can be used all year round. In the lounge, a fireplace also offers cozy warmth.

GETTING AROUND. PURA COMPORTA IS AN ARCHITECTURALLY DESIGNED HOLIDAY ESCAPE LOCATED AN HOUR SOUTH OF PORTUGAL'S CAPITAL, LISBON. PURA COMPORTA SITS ON A SANDY HILL STRADDLED BY DUNES AND GREEN FLOODPLAINS ON A WILD STRETCH OF PORTUGAL'S WEST COAST KNOWN AS THE ALENTEJO. RICE FARMERS, FISHERMEN, AND SALT FARMERS HAVE WORKED IN THE REGION FOR CENTURIES. CANALS CRISSCROSS LUSH RICE FIELDS, AND FLAMINGOS AND STORKS PEPPER THE WETLANDS. DESCRIBED IN TRAVEL GUIDES AS A PRISTINE SECRET PARADISE, COMPORTA AND ITS SURROUNDINGS ARE COVERED BY ENVIRONMENTAL PROTECTION LAWS AND REMAIN RESISTANT TO URBANIZATION. BAREFOOT WALKS AND BIKE RIDES ARE THE BEST MODES OF TRANSPORT IN THIS LANGUID PART OF THE WORLD WHERE SLOWNESS IS EMBRACED.

Exterior view of Pura Comporta with swimming
pool. Floor plan. Roof detail.

Interior view of a bedroom with large
panoramic window. Living area.
View of the kitchen with large cooking island.

Map of France, Portugal and Spain

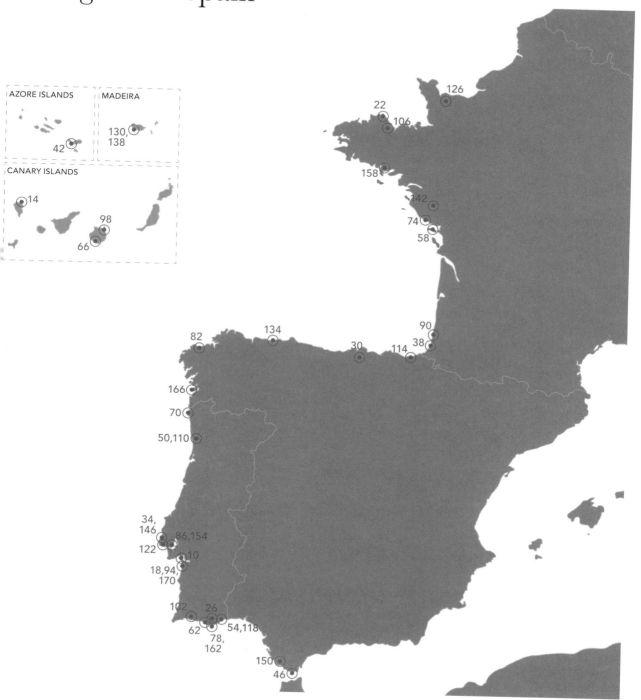

Picture
Credits

Oriane Badoual 107 a., 109 l.
Frederic Baron 23 b., 24, 25 b. r.
BCDF Studio, Paris 38 r., 39–40
Alexander Bogorodskiy Architectural
Photographer 162–165
Vanessa Bosio, Paris 74–77
Sarah Caglione 106, 107 b., 108, 109 r.
José Campos - Photographer
50–53, 70–73
Ana Paula Carvalho
118 a.l. and b., 120
Casa do Pego 94–97
Casa Shelly 150–153
Cédric Chasse 58–61
Mathieu Choiselat, Biarritz 38 l.
Teresa Correa 98–101
Luís da Cruz 102–105
Guilherme da Rosa 78–81
Susanna Falk 126 a. l. and b.,
128, 129 a. l. and b.
Sergio Fandino Sotelo 166 a.l.
Luís Ferraz 110–113
FG + SG Fotografia de Arquitectura
10–13
Floatel 14–17
Morgane Fouezon 22, 23 a.,
25 a.l., b. l. and a. r.
Nelson Garrido 18–21
Michel Gasser, La Rochbeblin 142–145
Fernando Guerra 42–45, 154–157,
138 a.l. and a. r., 139 l.,
140, 141 r., 170–173
Daniel Hernandez Padrón 66–69
Imagen Subliminal 114–117
Renée Kemps 88, 89 a. l. and a. r.

Philippa Langley 86 a. r.
Gaëlle Le Boulicaut 158 a. l. and a. r.,
159 r., 160, 161 a. r., b. r.
Miguel Manso 118 a.r., 119, 121
Christina Mendi 130–133
David Montero 30–33
Mr. Tripper 90–93
Francisco Nogueira 54–57, 62–65
OUTPOST Rodrigo Cardoso
34–37, 146–149
Nolwenn Pernin 126 a. r., 127, 129 a. r.
Diana Quintela 122–125
André Raibaut 158 b., 159 l., 161 l.
Alex Reyto 26–29,
86 a. l. and b., 87, 89 b.
Luis Santullano 134–137
Ciro Frank Schiappa, Barcelona
166 b. r., 167–168, 169 a. l.
Ocho Segundos, Vigo 169 a. l. and a. r
Tarifa Beach Houses 46–49
Michael Taylor 138 b., 139 r., 141 l.
VILANOVAA 82–85

All other pictures were made available
by the architects, designers, or hosts.

Cover front: Floatel
Cover back (from left to right, from
above to below): Tarifa Beach Houses,
Sarah Caglione, OUTPOST
Rodrigo Cardoso, FG + SG Fotografia
de Arquitectura